DISCARDED

BRANTFORD PUBLIC LIBRARY
3 5154 00457 811

D1477966

COUNTERTERRORISM
AND IDENTITIES

DISC

COUNTERTERRORISM AND IDENTITIES
Canadian Viewpoints

JACK JEDWAB

Copyright 2015 © Jack Jedwab and the Association of Canadian Publishers

All rights reserved. No part of this book may be reproduced, for any reason or by any means without permission in writing from the publisher.

Cover and book design: Paula Provost
Printed and bound in Canada.

Library and Archives Canada Cataloguing in Publication

Jedwab, Jack, 1958-, author
Counterterrorism and identities : Canadian viewpoints / Jack Jedwab.
Includes bibliography and references. Issued in print and electronic formats.

ISBN 978-1-927535-86-8 (paperback).--ISBN 978-1-927535-87-5 (epub).

ISBN 978-1-927535-88-2 (mobi).--ISBN 978-1-927535-89-9 (pdf)

1. National security--Canada--Public opinion. 2. Terrorism--Public
opinion. 3. Terrorism--Prevention--Public opinion. 4. Canada--Defenses--
Public opinion. 5. Public opinion--Canada. I. Title.

UA600.J43 2015   355'.033071   C2015-903424-8
                                             C2015-903425-6

The publisher gratefully acknowledges the support of SODEC for its publishing program.

Linda Leith Publishing Inc.
P.O. Box 322, Victoria Station
Westmount QC H3Z 2V8
Canada
www.lindaleith.com

CONTENTS

INTRODUCTION

The threat of terrorism cannot be understood in a vacuum. Increasingly, counterterrorism strategists recognize that circumstances and context matter when it comes to comprehending the conditions within which acts of terrorism occur. The way an analyst characterizes or defines the threat of terrorism frequently plays a critical role in determining the best response.

Achieving success in counterterrorism often depends on the degree of cooperation across government and community, and therefore requires effective commitment and participation from a wide range of actors. A high level of institutional trust on the part of an informed and alert public can be helpful. The public perception of the threat of terrorism and how it understands the issues underlying the threat are also useful in establishing optimal conditions for security officials as they choose a particular course of action. An ill-informed public with a high level of anxiety about security can be an impediment to effective counterterrorism.

Counterterrorism measures require that there be a delicate balance between what the "informed" public needs to know about a specific threat and what the public does not need to know. The degree of disclosure can be important in terms of the intelligence gathering that is so essential to effective counterterrorism. Insufficient disclosure about threats of terrorism may result in a breakdown in communication with the population, which may have a detrimental effect on public support for those responsible for the safety of society. The potential result will be lower perceived effectiveness in the fight against terrorism and a potential undercutting of the population's resilience in the aftermath of a terrorist incident.

Our identities matter. Counterterrorism strategists generally regard identities as important when establishing the profile of individuals or groups that commit acts of terrorism. Issues of identity play a larger role in understanding the context within which security concerns evolve. Effective counterterrorism frequently involves careful interaction between communities and those individuals tasked with protecting our security. This requires a good comprehension of the dynamics within which certain communities operate, as well as sensitivity to their concerns on the part of security officials. Establishing relationships of trust is very important. The ability of policing officials to work constructively with citizens is vital for success in the fight against counterterrorism.

To what extent are citizen anxieties about security and terrorism shaped by their identities? On a related question, do our social (i.e., age and gender) and cultural identities (i.e., ethnicity and religion) affect the preferred strategies and desired methods in the fight against terrorism? It is also important to consider the dominant markers of identity and the nature of identity-based tension and conflict. Nothing good can come from attaching stigmas to certain expressions of identity.

Exploring these and several related issues is a main objective of this book. *Counterterrorism and Identities: Canadian Viewpoints* seeks to improve our understanding of the societal context within which terrorist acts occur. With the support of Public Safety Canada's Kanishka Project, the Association for Canadian Studies (ACS) has compiled the largest bodies of survey data in the country on security, terrorism, and counterterrorism. This data offers insight into Canadian views on the basis of a wide range of demographic characteristics, including region of residence, age, gender, and religious identification.

This in-depth investigation looks at such considerations as Canadians' definition of terrorism, their level of anxiety about the phenomenon, their perceptions of the effectiveness of government initiatives to combat terrorism, what they regard as the sources of terrorism, their views around how security threats affect inter-communal harmony, who they would turn to in the event of a terrorist threat, who they regard as best positioned to deal with the threat of terrorism, and their willingness to sacrifice civil liberties in the fight against terrorism.

On these and several related issues, the Association has since 2012 commissioned the firm Leger Marketing to conduct surveys that monitor changes in public opinion and establish benchmarks, allowing us to measure the significance of a particular shift. To take one example, we establish the average level of anxiety felt by Canadians over terrorism and how this anxiety level is affected by terrorist events. By correlating responses to different questions, we can look into Canadian views on a variety of key issues as seen by those Canadians that are most and least anxious about terrorism in Canada and elsewhere in the world. The ten surveys that are central to the analysis were conducted via Web panel and, as they are not randomized, are characterized as having a probabilistic or estimated margin of error. The national surveys have had a minimum number of 1500 respondents excluding oversamples. Two of the surveys included oversamples of Muslims and Jews, and these provide valuable insights into how these minorities assess issues associated with terrorism and counterterrorism.

As they develop short and long term policies and programs aimed at combating terrorism, policymakers, policing officials, and researchers can benefit from the information and analyses in this publication. While making myriad observations based on the data, we invite readers to identify and recommend any key questions that we have missed in assembling the data.

My thanks to the Kanishka Project of Public Safety Canada and particularly to Brett Kubicek for his unwavering commitment to research in this vital area. The opinions offered here are mine alone and do not reflect the views of Public Safety Canada. Finally, a special thanks to Ashley Manuel of the Association for Canadian Studies for her dedication and assistance with the publication.

Jack Jedwab
President
Association for Canadian Studies and the
Canadian Institute for Identities and Migration

CHAPTER 1

UNDERSTANDING TERRORISM AND ITS "CAUSES"

Canada's *Criminal Code* defines terrorism *as:*

> ... an act or omission undertaken, inside or outside Canada, for a political, religious or ideological purpose that is intended to intimidate the public with respect to its security, including its economic security, or to compel a person, government or organization (whether inside or outside Canada) from doing or refraining from doing any act, and that intentionally causes one of a number of specified forms of serious harm. (Government of Canada, 2013, p. 6)

The United Nations abandoned its own attempt to define terrorism when some countries responsible for establishing the definition were perceived to be carrying out terrorist activities themselves. Nonetheless, common key descriptors used to define terrorism include "violence," "threat," "political," and "power." Terrorism is also always a systematic, planned, and calculated act (Hoffman, 1998). Although such definitions allow for the inclusion of a wide range of perpetrators, such as governments or religious groups, we must be mindful of the risks associated with broad definitions.

In his publication *Root Causes of Terrorism: Myths, Reality, and Ways Forward*, Bjørgo (2005) points out that researchers have circulated as many as two hundred definitions of terrorism. Yet he contends that among researchers as well as governments, there is tacit agreement that the core meaning of the concept of terrorism is "a set of methods or strategies of combat rather than an identifiable ideology or movement," and that "terrorism involves premeditated use of violence against (at least primarily) non-combatants in order to achieve a psychological effect of fear on others than the immediate targets."

Some definitions specifically exclude state actors as possible terrorists, whereas others include states. Some definitions restrict the notion of terrorism to attacks on civilians only, whereas other definitions would include military and police targets under non-war conditions. Some limit terrorism to violent acts with a political purpose, whereas others also include terrorism for criminal purposes.

When it comes to defining terrorism, it might be contended that a consensus has formed that there is no consensus. Some experts insist that due to its malleability and highly contentious nature, terrorism is open to various interpretations and definitions (Staiger, Letschert, Pemberton, and Ammerlaan, 2008; Weinberg, Pedahzur, and Hirsch-Hoefler, 2004; Fletcher, 2006).

CANADIAN DEFINITIONS OF TERRORISM

How do Canadians define terrorism? When asked to do so in one sentence, they offer a varied number of responses. As seen in Table 1, the majority of Canadians are unable to offer a definition or simply refuse to provide one. Amongst those who do respond, most understand terrorism to be the use of force or violence to support political/religious ideologies or a particular set of

JACK JEDWAB

values. Violence is a word that is evoked in conjunction with the definition of terrorism across the age spectrum.

Still, diverging views among younger and older Canadians remain an important consideration, with Canadians under the age of 45 somewhat less inclined to provide any definition. Older Canadians seem more inclined to define terrorism as the imposition of one's values/beliefs on others through the use of violence/coercion, or more simply as the use of force/violence motivated by religion/religious beliefs.

Perhaps the most important takeaway from Table 1 is that the more Canadians offer some definition (moving out of the "don't know" category), the more they see terrorism as the use of violence to impose one's values/beliefs on others.

TABLE 1 : CANADIANS DEFINE TERRORISM IN ONE SENTENCE

Define terrorism as:	Age					
	18-24	25-34	35-44	45-54	55-64	65+
I don't know/Prefer not to answer	41%	38%	40%	34%	37%	25%
The use of force/violence to instigate fear among a group or individuals	9%	13%	12%	9%	7%	7%
The use of force/violence for political objectives/ideology	8%	9%	8%	7%	8%	7%

COUNTERTERRORISM AND IDENTITIES : CANADIAN VIEWPOINTS

Define terrorism as:	Age					
	18-24	25-34	35-44	45-54	55-64	65+
Acts of violence against a group/nation/state	7%	5%	3%	3%	3%	4%
The use of force/violence motivated by religion/religious beliefs	6%	7%	9%	10%	16%	13%
The imposition of your values/beliefs on others through the use of violence or coercion	4%	6%	3%	8%	8%	17%
Evil/hate/bad/awful/horror/cruelty/inhuman	4%	3%	7%	1%	1%	2%
The killing/harming of innocent people Acts of violence committed by a minority/group towards a perceived threat or oppressor	3%	4%	5%	8%	7%	10%
Acts of violence committed by a minority/group towards a perceived threat or oppressor	3%	2%	2%	4%	1%	2%
Ridiculous/ignorant/crazy/manipulated people	3%	1%	0%	2%	2%	5%
Acts of random violence	2%	3%	3%	3%	6%	3%

Source: ACS-Leger Marketing, November 2012

8

JACK JEDWAB

PERCEIVED CAUSES OF TERRORIST ACTIVITIES

Bjørgo notes that in the aftermath of the attacks at the World Trade Centre on September 11, 2001, and with the declaration of the "War on Terrorism," some may find it irrelevant and potentially apologetic to speak about the "root causes" of terrorism. For those who subscribe to this view, terrorism is an evil that should not be rationalized and must be eradicated.

Others believe that it is essential to comprehend the context in which terrorism arises and consider that those who dismiss an inquiry into "root causes" risk being ill-equipped to respond when further terrorist incidents occur.

Carment and Prest (2013) contend that those who dismiss the "root causes" argument misunderstand both the scope of Canadian policy and the underlying causes of terrorism. They refer us to a statement by a former head of the World Bank, James Wolfensohn, speaking about the need for a global strategy designed to address "the root causes of terrorism: those of economic exclusion, poverty and under-development" (Carment and Prest, para. 7). They further point to studies on Canadians involved in international terrorism, showing that a sense of exclusion, marginalization, and political grievance are often key facets of "homegrown" terrorist behaviour. However, Carment and Prest also refer to a study conducted by the Canadian Security and Intelligence Services (CSIS), which reveals that even "well-integrated" (however defined) Canadian citizens — mainly young men — can be radicalized.

When it comes to the issue of root causes driving terrorism, the bottom line is that some people feel that there are such causes, while others disagree. In *Exploring the "Root Causes" of Terrorism*, Newman (2006) contends that the very idea of root causes suggests that there is some degree of causality between underlying social, political, economic and demographic conditions

9

and terrorist activities. According to this proposition, certain underlying conditions and grievances always explain how, where, and why terrorism arises. Failing to make such links results in ineffective approaches to counterterrorism. Newman declares that while root causality possesses some intuitive appeal, it is methodologically problematic and most analysts have therefore been hesitant to apply or test it.

We asked Canadians what they regard as the two most important factors contributing to terrorist actions. Three options were presented, based off a previously-asked open question, where there were no suggested responses. Religious motivation/fundamentalism, foreign policy, and poverty and economic inequality were the most common unprompted answers provided by respondents. When identifying what Canadians believe to be the two most important factors contributing to terrorist actions, it might be assumed that those attributing terrorist actions to fundamentalism are less likely to subscribe to the notion of root causes than those Canadians pointing to poverty and inequality as the key determinants.

Canadians appear very divided between religious fundamentalism and poverty and economic inequality as the main contributing factors to terrorist actions. Hence, there is no consensus amongst Canadians that root causes underlie terrorist actions. It is also fair to note that those who select economic inequality first most often offer Western foreign policy as a second explanation and far less frequently evoke religious fundamentalism.

As seen in Chart 1, there are important differences on the basis of age in response to the question of principal factors contributing to terrorist actions. The youngest group is more inclined to select poverty and inequality as the main contributor while the oldest cohort believes it is religious fundamentalism.

CHART 1 : THE TWO MOST IMPORTANT FACTORS THAT CONTRIBUTE TO TERRORIST ACTIONS (INITIAL RESPONSE ONLY)

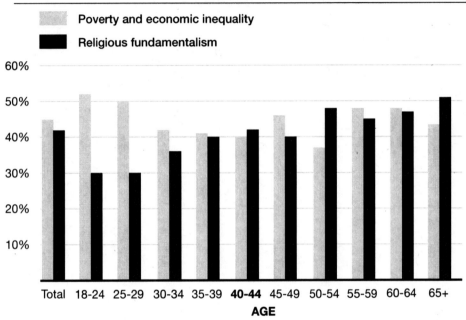

Source : ACS-Leger Marketing, November 2012

Chart 2 demonstrates the important difference between Muslims and non-Muslims asked to identify the most important factor(s) that contribute to terrorist actions. Canadian Jews and Christians were far more likely than Muslim Canadian respondents to identify religious fundamentalism as the principal contributing factor explaining terrorist actions; they selected this cause to a higher degree than they did poverty and economic inequality or Western foreign policy.

CHART 2 : THE TWO MOST IMPORTANT FACTORS THAT CONTRIBUTE TO TERRORIST ACTIONS (COMBINED PERCENTAGE)

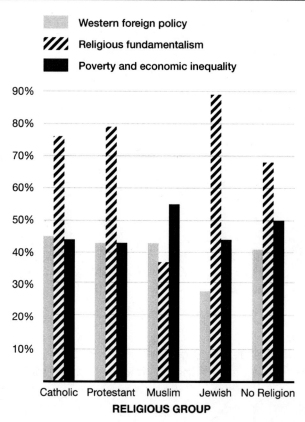

Source : ACS-Leger Marketing, March 2013

Since there is more than one form of terrorism, there are different motivations with divergent "causes." Terrorist incidents take place both in wealthier and poorer nations and in democracies as well as non-democratic regimes. Bjørgo suggests that there is a need to address whether the concept of "root causes of terrorism" is really useful. He points out that the notion of root causes is part of contemporary political discourse and does not arise from any empirical research on terrorism or other evidence-based studies offered by contemporary social theorists. It's simply assumed to be a sort of truism that no long-term success in the "War on Terrorism" can be expected as long as its root causes remain. Thus it is assumed that the removal of the root causes will put an end to terrorism. However, a deeply rooted problem of poverty can lead to a wide range of social justice concerns and it is less than apparent that terrorism is an inevitable outcome. In short, the cause and effect between poverty and terrorism is too often assumed rather than proven.

CAN TERRORISM BE JUSTIFIED UNDER SOME CIRCUMSTANCES?

Canadians may seem divided as to whether there are root causes behind terrorist actions, but this runs somewhat counter to the overwhelming degree to which Canadians affirm that acts of terrorism cannot be justified under any circumstances. Nearly nine in ten Canadians agree that terrorism cannot be justified under any circumstances. Less than 10 percent feel that under certain circumstances it can be justified, with a few others either saying they don't know or refusing to respond. While Muslim Canadians are somewhat less likely to agree that terrorism cannot be justified under any circumstances, the difference is relatively insignificant (Chart 3).

CHART 3 : EXTENT TO WHICH CANADIANS AGREE THAT TERRORISM CANNOT BE JUSTIFIED UNDER ANY CIRCUMSTANCES

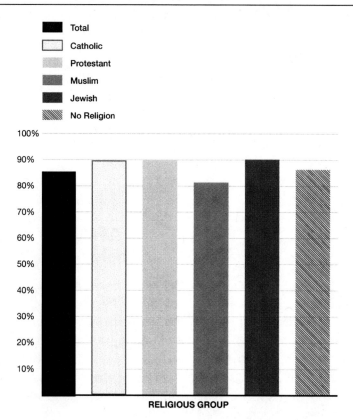

Source : ACS-Leger Marketing, March 2013

Primoratz (2013) argues that terrorism is wrong in itself, for it violates some of our most important rights and constitutes a grave injustice. Still, recourse to it may be morally permissible if a people or a political community finds itself *in extremis* and terrorism is the only way out. But then, just when are a people or a polity *in extremis*? Terrorism is *almost* absolutely wrong, and may be considered only (i) in the face of a "moral disaster," understood in a special, highly restrictive sense: as an imminent threat of extermination or ethnic cleansing of an entire people, and (ii) when there are good reasons to believe that terrorism is the only way of preventing the disaster, stopping it in its tracks or reversing a wide range of its consequences.

This definition seems close to what most Canadians are saying, even if some may see it as ambiguous. As revealed in Chart 4, even if Canadians think there are causes or social/economic explanations behind terrorist actions, they generally do not feel that such actions can be justified. Whether they believe that terrorist actions are principally attributed to economic inequality or religious fundamentalism, some 90 percent of Canadians do not feel that it can be justified.

CHART 4 : CORRELATION : PERCENTAGE OF THOSE WHO
AGREE THAT TERRORISM CANNOT BE JUSTIFIED UNDER ANY
CIRCUMSTANCES AS SEEN BY THOSE WHO REGARD EITHER POVERTY
AND ECONOMIC INEQUALITY OR RELIGIOUS FUNDAMENTALISM
AS MAIN FACTORS EXPLAINING TERRORIST ACTIONS

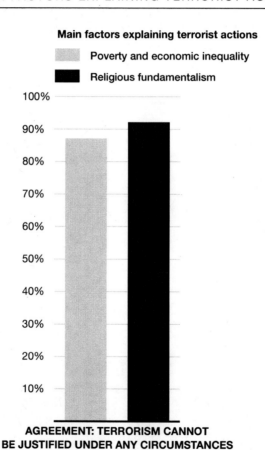

Main factors explaining terrorist actions

Poverty and economic inequality

Religious fundamentalism

**AGREEMENT: TERRORISM CANNOT
BE JUSTIFIED UNDER ANY CIRCUMSTANCES**

Source : ACS-Leger Marketing, March 2013

It is likely that to ignore the motivation behind terrorist attacks and the specific profile of terrorists — that is to singularly dismiss the "why" in looking at such acts — risks depriving those engaged in counterterrorism with essential information. In short, it is an oversimplification to say that it's a waste of time to study cause and causality when it comes to terrorism. At the same time, it is also an oversimplification to insist that incidences of terrorism inevitably involve some deeply rooted motive connected with economic and social vulnerability or exclusion.

CHAPTER 2

IDENTITIES

Growing ethnic diversity in countries such as Canada has generated two intersecting policy debates that cannot be overlooked, particularly when examining counterterrorism approaches (Soroka, Johnston, and Banting (2007).

The first of these debates celebrates diversity and challenges governments to respect cultural differences and construct inclusive forms of citizenship. The other emphasizes social cohesion or social integration, where the objective facing diverse societies is to strengthen a shared sense of community and construct a common national identity, especially important during times of insecurity. Policy orientation has shifted back and forth between these two debates of internal diversity versus national identity, but Soroka, Johnston, and Banting do not see any logical reason as to why both these agendas cannot be pursued amongst citizens simultaneously.

Pluralistic societies like Canada increasingly acknowledge multiple identifications, as Canadians possess various identities and attachments. In multicultural societies, we tend to think of identities as complementing one another rather than competing with one another. Even in Canada, however, debates around whether identities, especially ethnic and national ones, are inevitably in conflict has pre-dated the introduction of multicultural discourse and policies, and these continue to be at the centre of debates between supporters and opponents of multiculturalism. (We'll return to this issue in Chapter 6).

JACK JEDWAB

The type of "identity measurements" employed is often dependent on a particular understanding of national identity. The preferred approach tends to be connected to whether a particular society's model of diversity sees ethnic and/or religious identification as conflicting with national identity. The most common type of identity measurement requires a ranking of the importance of various expressions of identity (i.e., which of the following is most important: your nation, province, ethnic and/or religious group). An alternative approach does not frame the options as competitive, but rather employs scale measurement (we call this the "relative response" as opposed to the "required response") so as to determine the degree of attachment or belonging to a particular expression of identity (i.e., rate on a scale from very strong to very weak how attached you are to your nation, province, ethnic and/or religious group, etc.). Such a line of questioning denies a need to make choices between identities, for they can be viewed as complementary. The interpretation of results arising from these methods of measurement can be crucial in debates around identity and values.

CANADIAN IDENTITIES IN ORDER OF IMPORTANCE

When ranking identities in order of importance, Chart 5 shows that most Canadians put their national identity in first place, with the exception of Quebec Francophones (who put language ahead) and Muslims (who put their religious group above country). Though Muslims pick religion when they're forced to rank, they exhibit a very strong sense of attachment to Canada. Religion finishes in second place for Jewish Canadians and in third place for Canadians whose first language is neither English nor French.

CHART 5 : CANADIAN IDENTITIES IN ORDER OF IMPORTANCE

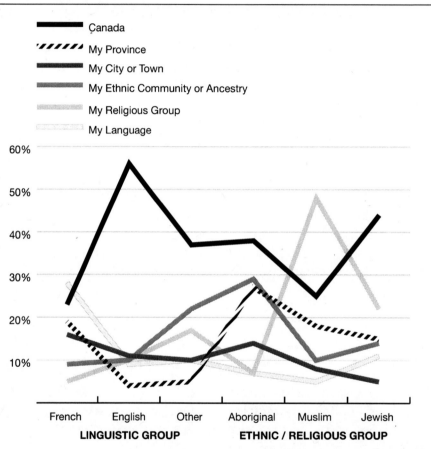

Source : ACS-Leger Marketing, January 2014

DEGREE OF CANADIAN ATTACHMENT TO MULTIPLE IDENTITIES

When considering the degree of attachment to various markers of identity in Chart 6, all groups of respondents exhibited a strong sense of attachment to Canada, with the sole exception of Quebec Francophones. Francophones rank provincial attachment higher than attachment to Canada. Attachment to religion ranks lower than all other expressions of identity for all language groups and aboriginals, but it is more important among Jews and Muslims. For the latter two religious groups, attachment to Canada is strongest.

CHART 6 : EXTENT TO WHICH CANADIANS ARE
ATTACHED TO SELECTED MARKERS OF IDENTITY

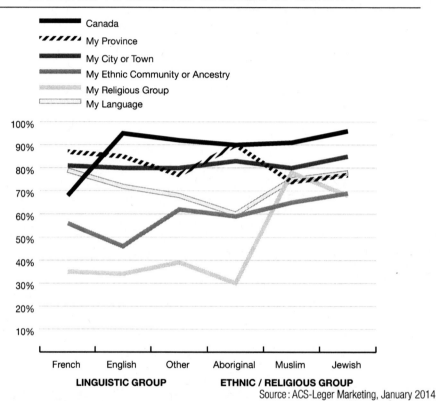

Source : ACS-Leger Marketing, January 2014

On the basis of age, in Chart 7, there is a large gap in the extent to which Canadians report that they are very attached to Canada. The younger age groups are much less likely to report that they are very attached to their country. Strong attachment to religion does somewhat better amongst the population over the age of 65, but nonetheless ranks lowest amongst Canadians when asked to identify those markers to which they are very attached.

CHART 7 : EXTENT TO WHICH CANADIANS ARE VERY ATTACHED TO SELECTED MARKERS OF IDENTITY

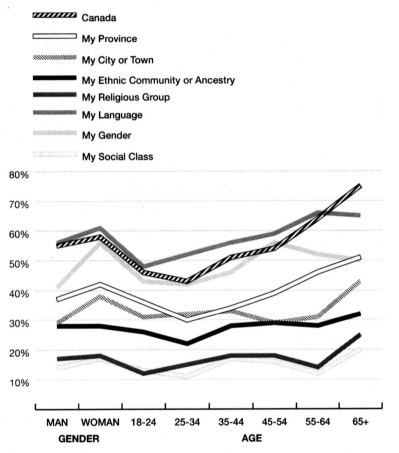

Source : ACS-Leger Marketing, November 2014

ARE IDENTITIES COMPETING ? RELIGION AND NATIONAL IDENTIFICATION

Even when not mentioned explicitly, it is religious identification that seems to be the focus in debates over identity and security. Very often such a linkage does not consider the role religion plays in people's lives. After all, identification with a religious group does not imply that adherence and practice are important to the individual. When the choice isn't forced, religious attachment does not undercut attachment to Canada. Indeed the data in Chart 8 reveals that the more someone is attached to their religious group, the more they are attached to Canada. This may seem counterintuitive to those who feel that Canadians must make a choice between identities, but the Canadian model does not require that such choices be made.

CHART 8 : CORRELATION : PERCENTAGE OF THOSE ATTACHED TO CANADA BY VARIOUS LEVELS OF ATTACHMENT TO RELIGIOUS GROUP

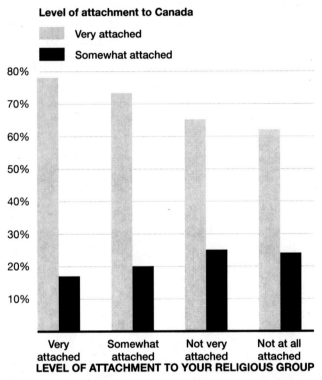

Level of attachment to Canada

Very attached

Somewhat attached

LEVEL OF ATTACHMENT TO YOUR RELIGIOUS GROUP

Source : ACS-Leger Marketing, March 2013

As regards specific religious groups in Chart 9, only in the case of Protestants do we find the least adherent being most attached to Canada. Predominantly, the older Catholic population, which tends to be Quebec Francophones, is more religious and more attached to Canada. As for Muslim and Jewish Canadians, the more attached they are to their religion, the more attached they are to Canada. There is little empirical evidence to support the affirmation that the salience of religion or religiosity is somehow undercutting national identity.

CHART 9 : CORRELATION : ATTACHMENT TO CANADA BY PERCENTAGE OF CANADIAN RELIGIOUS GROUPS ON THE BASIS OF ATTACHMENT TO RELIGIOUS GROUP

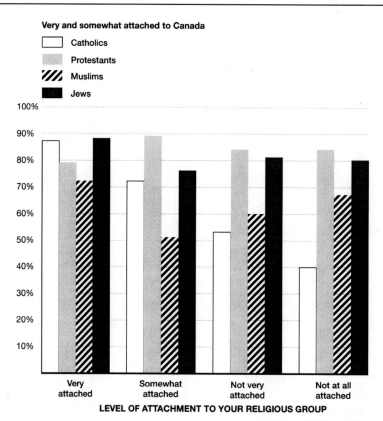

Source : ACS-Leger Marketing, March 2013

VALUES, IDENTITY, AND SECURITY

In some states, questions of identity and values are conflated with discussions of social cohesion. In turn, issues of national security are thought to be linked to the degree of social cohesion — a term that is often vaguely defined. In the aftermath of the terrorist attacks in January 2015 at the offices of Charlie Hebdo and the Hyper Cacher supermarket in Paris, there were widespread calls for intercultural harmony and greater cohesion across France and abroad. On several occasions, high level political discourse has made the link between identity, values, and national security. As the United Kingdom prepares its fall 2015 Counter-extremism Strategy, Prime Minister David Cameron affirmed that the strongest weapon against extremism is the nation's own liberal values. Indeed, his rationale for the adoption of the Counter-extremism Strategy is replete with references to values. For example he declared that:

> ... the bigotry, aggression and theocracy of terrorists need to be confronted with our values ... We are all British. We respect democracy and the rule of law. We believe in freedom of speech, freedom of the press, freedom of worship, equal rights regardless of race, sex, sexuality or faith. We believe in respecting different faiths but also expecting those faiths to support the British way of life. These are British values....
> Whether you are Muslim, Hindu, Jewish, Christian, or Sikh, whether you were born here or born abroad, we can all feel part of this country — and we must now all come together and stand up for our values with confidence and pride. Too often we have lacked the confidence to enforce our values, for fear of causing offence ...
> We can't expect them to see the power and liberating force of our values if we don't stand up for them when they come under attack ... and we are keeping up the pressure on cultural practices that can run

directly counter to these vital values....

We need everyone — government, local authorities, police, schools, all of us — to enforce our values right across the spectrum. (Dearden, 2015)

On the welcome page of the website of the Supreme Court of Canada, Chief Justice of Canada Beverley McLachlin (2015) points out that "much of our collective sense of freedom and safety comes from our community's commitment to a few key values: democratic governance, respect for fundamental rights and the rule of law, and accommodation of difference. Our commitment to these values must be renewed on every occasion, and the institutions that sustain them must be cherished" (para. 1).

Heath (2003) contends that values frequently get defined in abstract ways like "sharing," "democracy," or "dialogue." When values are defined in abstract terms, sharing them is relatively uncomplicated. He argues that "the governing principles of our political institutions are provided, not by some set of shared values, but rather by the goal of providing a framework that will be neutral with respect to controversial questions of value" (p. 3).

Attention is increasingly being directed at the perceived need to reconcile the values held by immigrants from non-democratic countries with those of the host society. Distinctions are frequently made between "their" values and "ours," with the former often vaguely referring to immigrants. A 2006 Environics survey shown in Chart 10 reveals that Canadians who strongly agree that there are too many immigrants coming into the country and not adopting Canadian values are most likely to agree with a ban on the wearing of head scarves by Muslim women, while those who disagree with the idea that immigrants are not adopting Canadian values would be least likely to support such a ban. We'll return to the issue of banning religious symbols in Chapter 7.

CHART 10 : 2006 ENVIRONICS SURVEY

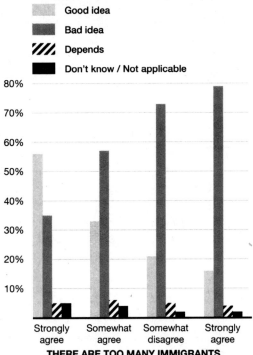

Some countries have decided to ban the wearing of head
scarves by Muslim women in public places, including schools.
Do you think this is a good idea or a bad idea?

- Good idea
- Bad idea
- Depends
- Don't know / Not applicable

**THERE ARE TOO MANY IMMIGRANTS
COMING INTO THIS COUNTRY WHO ARE
NOT ADOPTING CANADIAN VALUES**

Source : Environics, Focus Canada (FC 64), December 2006

Heath maintains that "shared values are neither necessary nor sufficient for social integration. Not only is the idea that we have shared values a myth, but the notion that we need such shared values is also a myth" (p. 7). In the pursuit of shared values, some will argue for limiting Charter rights (i.e., to freedom of religion or expression) while others will argue that in defence of shared values, it is necessary to be vigilant in the face of potential rights violations.

Ranier Baubock observes that "values and identity are often mentioned together so that they appear as interchangeable." He contends that "democratic values are said to provide the only defensible basis for national identity in societies of immigration, and, conversely, national identities in Western societies are seen as profoundly shaped by a common belief in democratic values" (Baubock, 2002, p. 2).

Undoubtedly, there is much rhetorical appeal in the framing of national identity debates on the basis of a set of shared values. Discussions of shared values are increasingly linked to debates over national identity. When terrorist incidents occur, some observers inevitably refer to a problem of shared values in society. Such discourse is in part a prime example of where security discourse intersects with identity debates.

Paradoxically, even those persons rejecting the notion of root causes seem swayed by the idea that at the core of the issue is a societal divide over values. In effect, it is not merely the values of the individual who commits terrorist acts, but that of the broader group with which such an individual is associated. Religious identification is the proverbial "elephant in the room" in this regard. Such associations are thoughtfully documented in essays published by Bramadat and Dawson (2014) in *Religious Radicalization and Securitization in Canada and Beyond.* The collection examines religious radicalization, its effect on minorities, increased securitization, and the efforts on the part of the public, media, and government to address the threat of radicalization and securitization.

Yet again, survey evidence provides little support for the idea that certain religious groups simply don't share our values. On the one hand, on the basis of religious identification in Chart 11, there is considerable agreement that such a thing as shared Canadian values do exist (presumably distinct from universal values).

CHART 11 : EXTENT TO WHICH CANADIANS AGREE
THAT THERE ARE SHARED CANADIAN VALUES

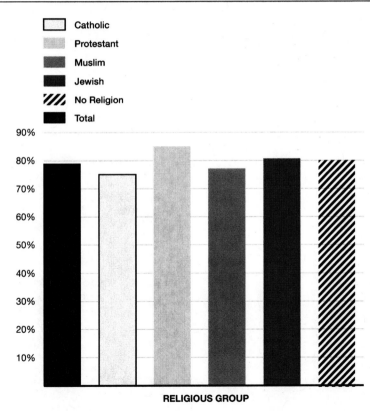

Source : ACS-Leger Marketing, March 2013

As observed in Chart 12, however, the majority identifying with the groups in the table below believe they share such Canadian values. Those persons identifying with "no religion" are least likely to agree that the values driving Canadian society are similar to their own.

CHART 12 : EXTENT TO WHICH CANADIANS AGREE THAT THE VALUES DRIVING CANADIAN SOCIETY ARE SIMILAR TO THEIR OWN

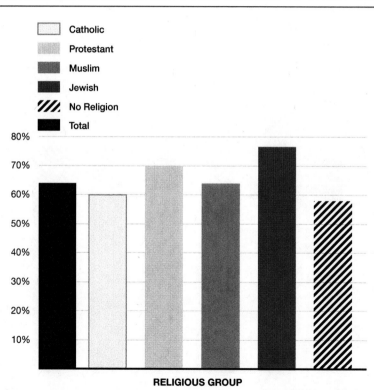

RELIGIOUS GROUP

Source : ACS-Leger Marketing, March 2013

Is there agreement on key issues between those Canadians who purport to share Canadian values and those who don't?

Well, there is no consensus over whether there should be complete separation of Church and state in Canada, whether or not you happen to agree there are shared Canadian values or if you attest to sharing them or not, as seen in Chart 13.

CHART 13 : CORRELATION : PERCENTAGE OF THOSE WHO AGREE THAT THERE SHOULD BE COMPLETE SEPARATION OF CHURCH AND STATE ON THE BASIS OF LEVELS OF AGREEMENT THAT THE VALUES DRIVING CANADIAN SOCIETY ARE SIMILAR TO THEIR OWN

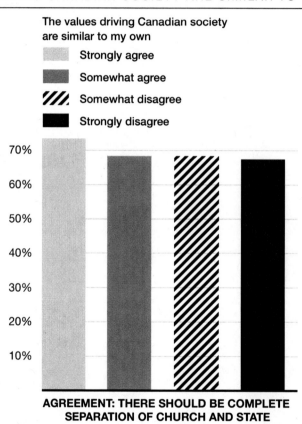

The values driving Canadian society are similar to my own

Strongly agree

Somewhat agree

Somewhat disagree

Strongly disagree

AGREEMENT: THERE SHOULD BE COMPLETE SEPARATION OF CHURCH AND STATE

Source : ACS-Leger Marketing, March 2013

There clearly are things that a majority of Canadians value. This does not imply that they are shared values. Such debates aside, Chart 14 demonstrates that the majority of Canadians believe that having many religious groups is an asset. Canadian Muslims and Jews are most likely to favour religious pluralism. At the same time, however, most believe that religion is divisive, with the exception of Muslim Canadians, where seven in ten agree that religion brings people together more than it divides them.

CHART 14 : EXTENT TO WHICH CANADIANS AGREE
IN SOCIETAL VALUES RELATED TO RELIGION

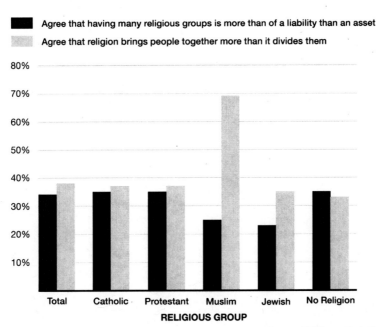

■ Agree that having many religious groups is more than of a liability than an asset

▨ Agree that religion brings people together more than it divides them

Source : ACS-Leger Marketing, March 2013

Lofty declarations that situate issues of security and the threat of terrorism as problems of national identity and / or a failure to inculcate shared national values may do more to stigmatize identifiable groups than advance social harmony. They also may serve to distract us from important and necessary discussions about the place of religion in society. Words matter. There is a definite need to reflect upon the discourse that is employed by opinion leaders when thinking about the relationship between identity and security.

CHAPTER 3

CANADIANS' SENSE OF SECURITY

Measuring the public's sense of security is a complex task. On the basis of nearly four years of survey results, we have attempted to identify a point of reference or benchmark against which measurement can be made. The benchmark for the state of anxiety about terrorism or perceived effectiveness in combating it is a fixed standard over a fixed time period, against which change can be assessed. This offers a basis for comparison at other points in time. When it comes to the public's sense of security, long-term trends in opinion are difficult to establish due to the impact of major events or incidents on attitudes towards security, terrorism, and counterterrorism. Trend analysis needs to compare opinions within the time-frame of a major incident as well as outside that period, so as to properly determine its impact on the public's perspective. This will be demonstrated over the course of this chapter.

A decade and a half following the tragic events of September 11, 2001, Canadians remain as concerned as ever by the threat of terrorism. Despite heightened security measures adopted by governments around the world where threats were perceived to be the strongest, concerns continue, especially as new threats such as the Islamic State (ISIS-ISIL) arise.

TERRORISM: THE THREATS FROM ABROAD

We have recently seen a significant exacerbation of tensions in Eastern Europe, the Middle East, and Asia. The military expansion of ISIS-ISIL, Russia's encroachment in the Ukraine, international exchanges regarding Iran's nuclear program, conflict between Israel and the Palestinians, and China's handling of pro-democracy protests have given rise to several important domestic decisions over foreign policy and highly charged debates in the Parliament of Canada. Regardless of the various contemporary sources for global tension and insecurity, Canadians continue to be most worried about the threat of Islamic fundamentalism, highlighted in Chapter 2 as the leading perceived cause of terrorism, followed by the development of nuclear weapons by Iran and the conflict between Russia and the Ukraine. The following list was derived primarily from a survey conducted by the firm Gallup, which asked Americans to offer a similar ranking in February of 2014.

When comparing various global security threats in Chart 15, it is the concern over Islamic fundamentalism that ranks highest. On the basis of language identification it is francophones that exhibit the highest degree of concern over Islamic fundamentalism.

CHART 15 : EXTENT TO WHICH CANADIANS ARE VERY WORRIED ABOUT THE FOLLOWING GLOBAL SECURITY THREATS, BASED ON LINGUISTIC GROUP

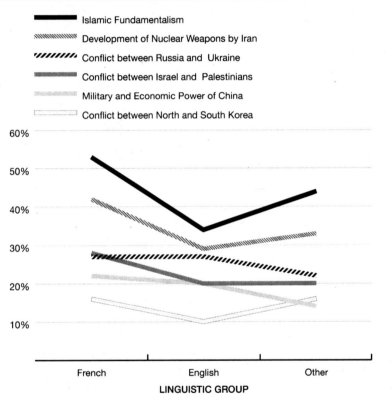

Source : ACS-Leger Marketing, September 2014

Chart 16 demonstrates how Islamic fundamentalism is also regarded as a greater threat by men and older Canadians.

CHART 16 : EXTENT TO WHICH CANADIANS ARE VERY WORRIED ABOUT THE FOLLOWING GLOBAL SECURITY THREATS, BASED ON GENDER AND AGE

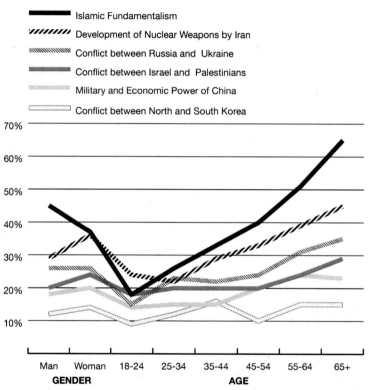

Source : ACS-Leger Marketing, September 2014

Most Canadians believe that conflicts are imported from abroad and that the domestic incidents of terrorism are a function of international influences. Accordingly, in Chart 17, we see that the majority of Canadians believe that historic conflicts that originate outside of Canada contribute to tensions between certain racial, religious, and cultural communities within Canada. The majority of Canadians find this concerning, as seen in Chart 18.

CHART 17 : EXTENT TO WHICH CANADIANS AGREE THAT HISTORIC CONFLICTS THAT ORIGINATE OUTSIDE OF CANADA CONTRIBUTE TO TENSIONS BETWEEN CERTAIN RACIAL, RELIGIOUS, AND CULTURAL COMMUNITIES IN CANADA

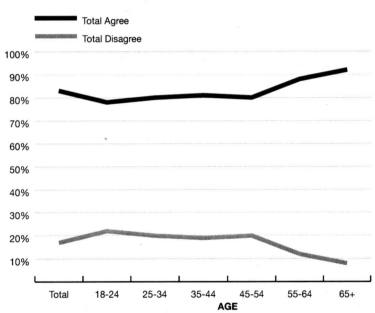

Source : ACS-Leger Marketing, March 2012

CHART 18 : EXTENT TO WHICH CANADIANS AGREE THAT THEY ARE CONCERNED WITH THE TENSIONS THAT ARISE FROM HISTORIC CONFLICTS THAT ORIGINATE OUTSIDE OF CANADA BETWEEN CERTAIN RACIAL, RELIGIOUS, AND CULTURAL COMMUNITIES IN CANADA

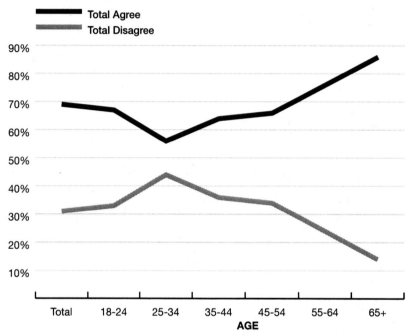

Source : ACS-Leger Marketing, March 2012

THE LINGERING SEPTEMBER 11 EFFECT

In the United States and elsewhere in the world, there is little doubt that the horrific events that occurred in New York City on September 11, 2001 (commonly referred to as 9/11), still very much influence the manner in which recent terrorist activities are interpreted and continue to have a considerable impact on levels of anxiety over the threat of terrorism.

According to Roxane Cohen Silver (2011), the attacks of 9/11 have tugged at society's social fabric and shattered a sense of security and perceptions of invulnerability amongst residents of the United States and the Western world. As such, it is not surprising that a majority of Canadians agree that the events of September 11 have modified their sense of security. As revealed in Chart 19, unsurprisingly the youngest cohort of Canadians are less inclined to indicate that they have been affected by the events of September 11, likely owing to the fact that their recollection of the event is not as strong. Canadian Jews are by far the most likely to indicate that the events of September 11 have changed their sense of security.

CHART 19 : EXTENT TO WHICH CANADIANS AGREE THAT THE EVENTS OF SEPTEMBER 11, 2001, HAVE CHANGED THEIR SENSE OF SECURITY

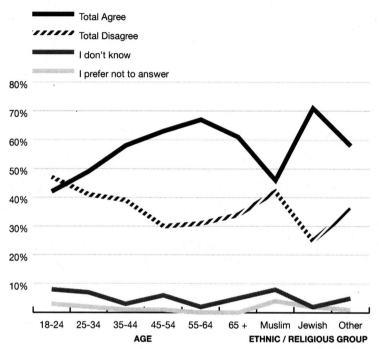

Source : ACS-Leger Marketing, January 2014

THE "NORMAL" LEVEL OF ANXIETY ?

As an emotion, anxiety is subjective and often associated with changes in feelings, behaviours, thoughts, and physiology. Like all emotional states, anxiety is experienced in varying levels of intensity. We all experience some degree of anxiety in our daily routine, and its expression varies for each individual. Lower degrees of anxiety are normal and adaptive. Anxiety is a normal response to stress and is linked to apprehension, uneasiness, and uncertainty. When anxiety rises above a "normal" level, some coping mechanisms may be needed. When it comes to collective anxiety over our security, it is often assumed that coping mechanisms will come from government or governing bodies, like police that are tasked with protecting our security.

According to Jacofsky, Santos, Khemlani-Patel, and Neziroglu (2013), "the most important distinction between fear and anxiety is the time-frame. Fear is the response to a danger that is *currently* detected in the immediate, *present* moment of time. In contrast, anxiety refers to the *anticipation* of some potential threat that may, or may not, happen in the *future*. In other words, *fear is a response to an immediate danger in the present moment of time, while anxiety is associated with a threat that is anticipated in a future moment of time*" (para. 3).

Acts of terrorism are designed to create disruption by instilling fear and anxiety in the public that lead to wide-ranging social, political, psychological, and economic consequences (Silver and Matthew, 2008). When governments warn the public about the possibility of a terror attack, observers will tend to express concern about the psychological consequences of causing such alarm (McDermott and Zimbardo, 2007).

As seen in Chart 20, the majority of Canadians are anxious about terrorist activities. In fact, the degree of concern expressed in September 2014 was seven points above the benchmark, and it is relatively safe to conclude that over the years, there has been a steady climb amongst those Canadians that say they are very worried about terrorism. In Canada, since such opinion is more likely to be affected by events outside the country, it might be concluded that the perceived rise in the intensity of conflicts occurring abroad is the source of higher degrees of anxiety amongst Canadians.

CHART 20 : CANADIANS' WORRY OVER TERRORISM

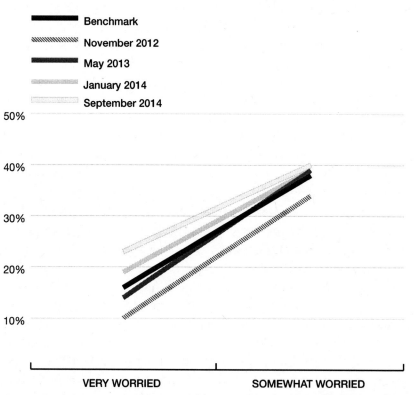

Source : ACS-Leger Marketing

Canadians are more concerned about terrorist activities in the world than about the threat of domestic terrorism, as depicted in Charts 21 and 22. This heightened level of concern with terrorism around the globe is especially apparent amongst the population above the age of 55. This finding supports the notion that Canadians regard terrorist action as something that is imported into Canada, rather than originating from within the country and described in the current vernacular as "home-grown." This is not to say that Canadians are not concerned with the domestic expression of terrorism. Recent high profile terrorist attacks in Canada's national capital and in Saint-Jean, Quebec, may indeed have modified relative levels of anxiety about terrorism here versus its incidence elsewhere in the world. To date, however, our survey findings suggest that greater anxiety is connected to perceptions of conflicts overseas.

Between January and September of 2014, as shown in Chart 21, there was an increase in concern about terrorist activities both in Canada and in the world. This has been more likely affected by events outside of the country, leading to the conclusion that the perceived rise in the intensity of conflicts occurring abroad is the source of higher degrees of anxiety here in Canada. However, there is an important difference in opinion on anxieties over terrorism in Canada or abroad when looking at both Chart 21 and Chart 22 on the basis of age, with the youngest group (18-24) seemingly much less worried about such activities when compared with persons above the age of 65.

CHART 21 : CANADIANS WORRIED ABOUT TERRORIST ACTIVITIES IN CANADA AND THE WORLD

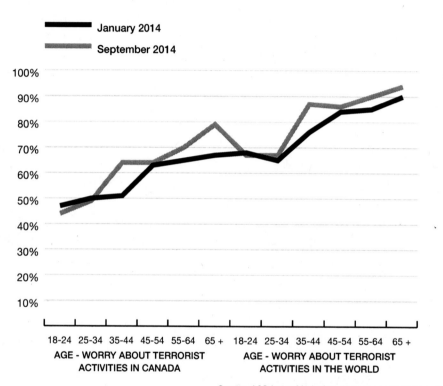

Source : ACS-Leger Marketing, January and September 2014

CHART 22 : CANADIANS VERY WORRIED ABOUT TERRORIST ACTIVITIES IN CANADA VERSUS THE WORLD

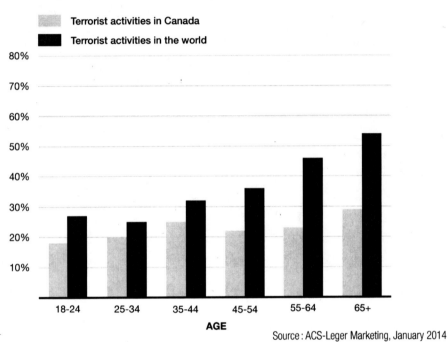

Source: ACS-Leger Marketing, January 2014

On the basis of religious identification in Chart 23, Canadians are more concerned about global terrorism relative to domestic terrorism. Jews are by far the most concerned with terrorism on an international scale.

CHART 23 : CANADIANS VERY AND SOMEWHAT WORRIED ABOUT TERRORISM IN CANADA AND THE WORLD, BASED ON RELIGIOUS IDENTIFICATION

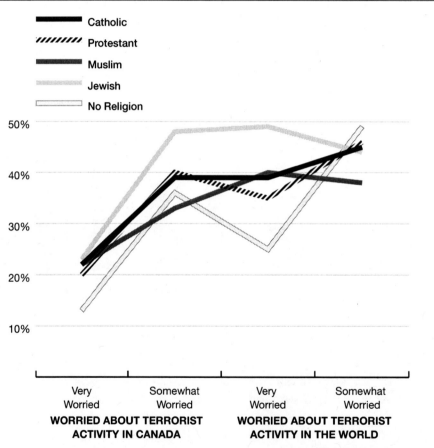

Source : ACS-Leger Marketing, March 2013

According to Chart 24, two-thirds of respondents believe that terrorists' ability to launch another major attack is greater today than ever before. There is a significant age gap in this belief, with the older cohort of Canadians agreeing with this statement.

CHART 24 : CANADIANS' BELIEF THAT THE ABILITY OF TERRORISTS TO LAUNCH ANOTHER MAJOR ATTACK IS GREATER TODAY THAN EVER

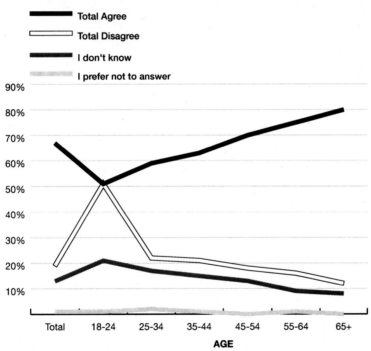

Source : ACS-Leger Marketing, September 2014

THE IMPACT OF THE MEDIA

As major sources of information about terrorism, the media are undoubtedly important drivers of public perceptions/anxieties. Looking at the principal news media in Chart 25, it is those respondents who most frequently watch television who exhibit the highest level of concern when it comes to terrorist activity and are most likely to agree that there is an irreconcilable conflict between Muslims and the West (a question that will be further explored in Chapter 5). The higher concern is in part attributable to the older audience that views television. But it is fair to observe that images to which there is greater exposure via television play an important role in opinion formation.

CHART 25 : HOW SOURCES OF NEWS IMPACT CANADIAN PERCEPTIONS

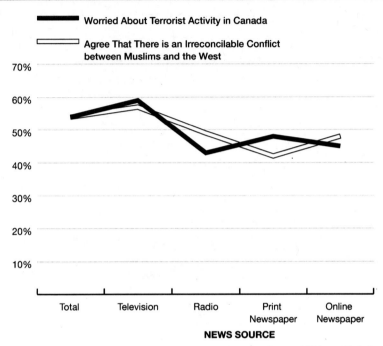

Source : ACS-Leger Marketing, March 2013

When looking at which of a series of selected television media draw higher rates of concern about terrorist activity in Chart 26, it is the French TVA network that has the highest overall percentage of Canadians very worried about terrorist activity. The English CTV network has the highest overall percentage of persons worried about terrorist activity within Canada.

CHART 26 : LEVEL WORRIED ABOUT TERRORISM, ON THE BASIS OF PRINCIPAL SOURCE FOR NEWS

TVA | 105 total respondents

CNN | 98 total respondents

GLOBAL NEWS | 72 total respondents

CTV | 186 total respondents

CBC | 191 total respondents

RDI | 86 total respondents

RADIO-CANADA | 80 total respondents

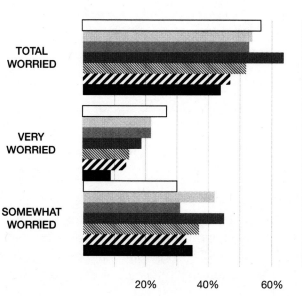

Source : ACS-Leger Marketing, March 2013

JACK JEDWAB

PERCEIVED EFFECTIVENESS IN THE FIGHT AGAINST TERRORISM

Perl (2007) contends that the perception and measure of progress in combating terrorism is important for the formulation and implementation of an anti-terror strategy. He adds that public perceptions can also have a major impact on how nations prioritize and allocate resources. Amongst the attitudinal criteria he cites, we find negative psychological or behavioural impact of terrorism on a society and the loss of public confidence in governments, or in their security measures, as particularly relevant.

With regards to the degree of effectiveness in combating terrorism by international authorities, perceptions amongst Canadians have evolved over the past few years as seen in Chart 27. Men are more likely than women to agree that international efforts to combat terrorism are working well. In September 2014, Canadians were six points below the benchmark (at 26%) in the extent to which they agreed that international efforts to combat terrorism were working well. There is a fairly consistent decline in the extent to which Canadians believe that international efforts are effective.

CHART 27 : EVOLUTION OF CANADIAN AGREEMENT THAT INTERNATIONAL EFFORTS TO COMBAT TERRORISM ARE WORKING WELL

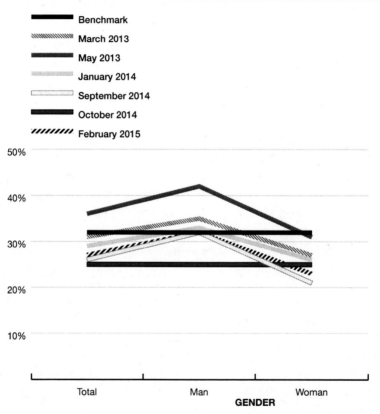

Source : ACS-Leger Marketing

As depicted in Chart 28, Muslim Canadians are somewhat more inclined than other groups surveyed to think that international efforts to combat terrorism are working well.

CHART 28 : EXTENT TO WHICH CANADIANS AGREE THAT
INTERNATIONAL EFFORTS TO COMBAT TERRORISM ARE WORKING WELL

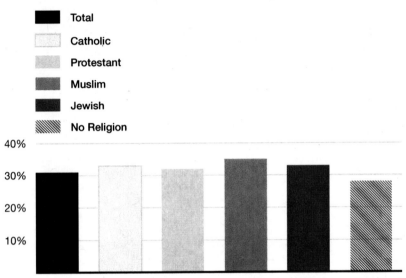

- Total
- Catholic
- Protestant
- Muslim
- Jewish
- No Religion

Source : ACS-Leger Marketing, March 2013

Canadians' perceptions have also evolved over the past few years with regard to the degree of effectiveness in combating terrorism by domestic authorities, as shown in Chart 29. Men are more likely than women to agree that the Government of Canada's efforts to combat terrorism are working well. In January and again in September 2014, the extent to which Canadians agree that efforts to combat terrorism are working well returned to the levels observed in March 2013 (38%), substantially lower than the percentage reported in May 2013 (51%), which came after the arrest of alleged bombers in Canada in connection with a plot against a national railway line. The shift in opinion suggests the importance of the effect that events can have in modifying public opinion.

CHART 29 : EVOLUTION OF CANADIAN AGREEMENT THAT THE GOVERNMENT OF CANADA'S EFFORTS TO COMBAT TERRORISM ARE WORKING WELL

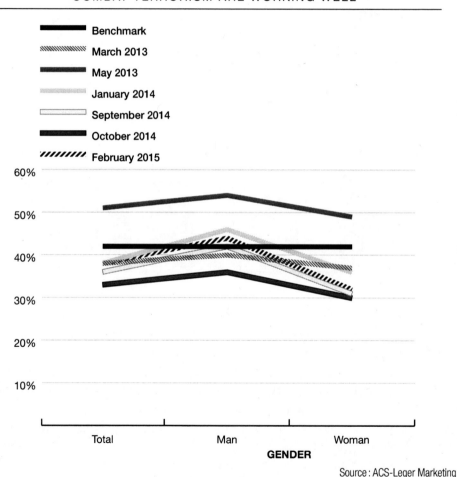

Source : ACS-Leger Marketing

In Chart 30, we see that fewer and fewer Canadians believe that terrorism has declined in the world over the course of the last decade. From an initial one-in-five Canadians to about one-in-eight agreeing, it's clear that most Canadians do not feel that terrorism is on the decline ; this is especially true of women.

CHART 30 : EVOLUTION OF CANADIAN AGREEMENT THAT TERRORISM HAS DECLINED IN THE WORLD OVER THE LAST DECADE

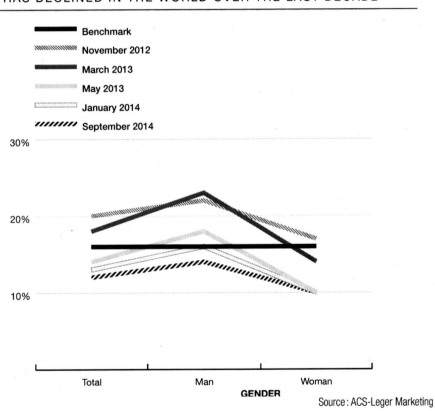

Source : ACS-Leger Marketing

Chart 31 shows that Muslim Canadian respondents are the most likely to agree that terrorism has declined in the world over the past decade, while Canadian Jews are the least likely to concur.

CHART 31 : EXTENT TO WHICH CANADIANS AGREE THAT TERRORISM HAS DECLINED IN THE WORLD OVER THE LAST DECADE

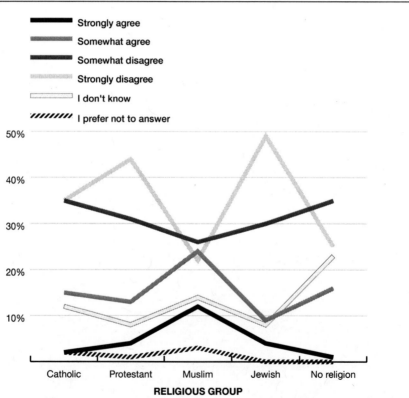

Source : ACS-Leger Marketing, March 2013

There does not appear to be anything particularly surprising in the finding that those of us who are more anxious about terrorist activities are more inclined to agree that terrorism is on the rise. Yet, as seen in Chart 32, some may be perplexed to discover that those Canadians who are more anxious about terrorism are far more likely to agree that government efforts to combat terrorism are working well, while those least anxious appear more dissatisfied with what is being done. In part, the explanation is that the least anxious feel that the government has gone too far in addressing the threat or has chosen the wrong strategy to do so.

CHART 32 : CORRELATION : PERCEIVED RISE IN TERRORISM AND CANADIAN GOVERNMENT EFFECTIVENESS IN COMBATING TERRORISM, AS SEEN BY THOSE VERY WORRIED AND NOT WORRIED AT ALL ABOUT TERRORIST ACTIVITIES IN CANADA

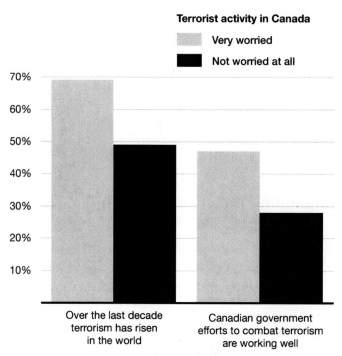

Source : ACS-Leger Marketing, March 2013

CHAPTER 4

COUNTER-TERRORISM

If most Canadians have difficulty even defining terrorism, they can't be expected to be very knowledgeable about counterterrorism. It may be surprising to learn that the degree of knowledge about counterterrorism is low given that terrorism is such a great a source of anxiety for so many Canadians. Both domestically and internationally, there is no shortage of information from the government and the media about terrorist incidents and counterterrorism policies and practices. The lack of knowledge is perhaps compounded by the fact that we assume that much counterterrorism activity is covert (we often acquire most of our knowledge of counterterrorism from Hollywood films).

As to the definition of counterterrorism, it has been succinctly regarded as the practices, tactics, techniques, and strategies that governments, militaries, and police departments adopt in response to terrorist threats and/or acts, both real and perceived. Some observers distinguish between soft and hard approaches to counterterrorism. Those advocating the softer solutions are somewhat more inclined to subscribe to the idea that the root causes of terrorism need to be identified and treated. Those supporting a harder line are somewhat more inclined to feel that terrorist acts are guided by ideology.

Former British Foreign Minister David Miliband contends that there is no military solution to terrorism. He believes that the post-9/11 war on terror has ultimately done more harm than good. He adds that this war has undermined the search for alternative, more successful approaches to countering violent extremism by giving the impression that only a military solution can be effective. Miliband points to the European Union and the United Nations rejection of a purely military approach as a solution to violent extremism — and their respective calls for a better understanding of the " conditions conducive to radicalisation and extremism that lead to terrorism" — as a prerequisite for developing effective counter-terrorism policies. He suggests that the United States has never bought into the soft approach and continues to follow a military strategy. That view is anchored in perception, as American counterterrorism strategies are far more complex than assumed and certainly not confined to military intervention (El-Said, 2015).

Governments are generally aware that how they choose to prevent terrorism either overseas or domestically and how they choose to assess their interventions is not only important to outcomes, but also to the legitimacy that the public accords to such interventions. Canada is no exception in this regard. Public Safety Canada has described the Canadian counterterrorism strategy as operating via four mutually reinforcing elements: *Prevent, Detect, Deny,* and *Respond* (Government of Canada, 2013). All government activity is directed towards one or more of these elements, which are defined as follows:

> *Prevent:* Activities in this area focus on the motivations of individuals who engage in, or have the potential to engage in, terrorist activity at home and abroad. The emphasis will be on addressing the factors that may motivate individuals to engage in terrorist activities.
>
> *Detect:* This element focuses on identifying terrorists, terrorist organizations and their supporters, their capabilities and the nature of their plans. This is done through investigation, intelligence operations, and

analysis, which can also lead to criminal prosecutions. Strong intelligence capabilities and a solid understanding of the changing threat environment is key. This involves extensive collaboration and information sharing with domestic and international partners.

Deny: Intelligence and law enforcement actions can deny terrorists the means and opportunities to pursue terrorist activities. This involves mitigating vulnerabilities and aggressively intervening in terrorist planning, including prosecuting individuals involved in terrorist related criminal activities, and making Canada and Canadian interests a more difficult target for would-be terrorists.

Respond: Terrorist attacks can and do occur. Developing Canada's capacities to respond proportionately, rapidly and in an organized manner to terrorist activities and to mitigate their effects is another aspect of the strategy. This element also speaks to the importance of ensuring a rapid return to ordinary life and reducing the impact and severity of terrorist activity.

CANADIAN KNOWLEDGE OF COUNTERTERRORISM APPROACHES

When Canadians were asked in an open question to identify two actions that Canada has taken over the past five years to combat terrorism, most respondents either did not know or refused to respond, as seen in Chart 33. The most common response amongst those that did offer an answer was enhancing airport security. The second most common reply was border security and patrols. The next most common response was military intervention abroad. The common denominator in these responses is the degree of visibility of the interventions that are identified by Canadians.

CHART 33 : CANADIANS IDENTIFY ACTIONS THAT CANADA HAS TAKEN OVER THE PAST FIVE YEARS TO COMBAT TERRORISM

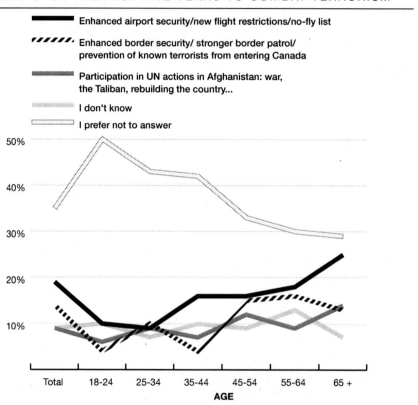

Source : ACS-Leger Marketing, November 2012

There is a difference between what Canadians purportedly know about counterterrorism initiatives and what they regard as the best methods for addressing terrorism. This gap is attributable to a lack of knowledge around what is being done. With regard to the best ways to fight terrorism, most

Canadians surveyed confess to being ignorant. But for those who do respond, there appears to be a slight preference for softer counterterrorism initiatives that focus on dialogue and education, as seen in Table 2. Out of the 50 percent surveyed who chose to respond, Canadians offer a wide range of suggested approaches running across a spectrum from the softer forms of outreach to harder repressive interventions.

That said, the expressed preference for softer approaches by no means implies disapproval of measures that are not on the top of the list. In other words, advocates of a tougher approach don't reject softer interventions (dialogue but not necessarily dialogue), while those favouring a softer stand don't exclude something tougher if needed (although they tend to support it to a lesser extent).

TABLE 2 : RANKING CANADIAN SUGGESTIONS AS TO THE BEST WAY TO FIGHT TERRORISM

1	Better dialogue / better communication / tolerance between cultures / different beliefs and religions
2	Better education for everyone (in the world) / to fight ignorance
3	Stricter immigration policies / make the immigrants respect our laws / our culture
4	Security measures / stricter laws / security at borders (including passports)

Source : ACS-Leger Marketing, March 2013

SOFT RATHER THAN HARD APPROACHES TO COUNTERTERRORISM

Canadians believe that reconciliation of differences on the basis of religious beliefs is an important element in addressing concerns around terrorism. Given this view, it is relatively safe to conclude that those favouring softer approaches to counterterrorism concur that religious ideology is a primary motivation of those engaged in terrorist actions. It is on this basis that it is further assumed that the remedy might arise from leaders of the relevant faith groups.

When it comes to issues of national security, Chart 34 shows that most Canadians believe that religion plays an important role, as evidenced by the belief that dialogue between religious officials (imams, priests, rabbis, etc.) is essential in combating the threat of terrorism. Older Canadians and Francophones are most inclined to assign value to such dialogue. So far as awareness of interfaith dialogue is concerned, fewer than one in four Canadians say they know about an initiative that promotes dialogue between different religious groups. Francophones are by far the least likely to be aware of any such activity. When it comes to potential interest in participating in such dialogue, some one in three Canadians express interest, with Francophones least likely to do so. This level of interest in participation in such dialogue is relatively high. A significant minority of Canadians agree that government should fund such dialogue.

CHART 34 : EXTENT TO WHICH CANADIANS
SUPPORT DIALOGUE APPROACHES

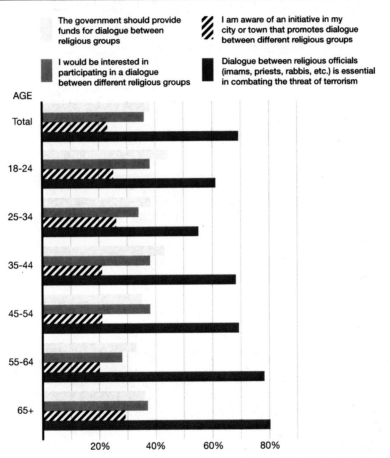

Source : ACS-Leger Marketing, March 2015

A pattern emerges in Table 3 when considering that those who believe economic vulnerability to be the most important factor that contributes to terrorist actions are also more inclined to support soft approaches. These respondents favour dialogue, as opposed to those who believe religious fundamentalism is principally behind terrorist action.

TABLE 3 : CORRELATION : PERCENTAGE OF THOSE WHO AGREE WITH VARIOUS WAYS TO FIGHT TERRORISM, RESPECTIVELY SEEN BY THOSE WHO AGREE THAT POVERTY AND ECONOMIC INEQUALITY AND RELIGIOUS FUNDAMENTALISM ARE THE MOST IMPORTANT FACTORS THAT CONTRIBUTE TO TERRORIST ACTIONS

Best way to fight terrorism	Most important factors that contribute to terrorist actions	
	Poverty and economic inequality	Religious fundamentalism
Better education for everyone (in the world)/ to fight ignorance	17%	10%
More social justice/ creating an equitable world	6%	1%
By funding and supporting economic development/ eliminate the large gap between rich and poor	5%	0%
Better dialogue/better communication/tolerance between cultures/different beliefs and religions	17%	12%

Best way to fight terrorism	Most important factors that contribute to terrorist actions	
	Poverty and economic inequality	Religious fundamentalism
By punishing them/ an eye for an eye	5%	6%
Stricter immigration policies/ make the immigrants respect our laws/ our culture	4%	15%
Security measures/ stricter laws/ security at borders (including passports)	5%	11%

Source: ACS-Leger Marketing, March 2013

Those who advocate soft approaches to counterterrorism are, as Table 4 shows, much less anxious about the domestic threat of terrorism relative to those Canadians endorsing a tougher stand on terrorism. Those who believe in the possibility of dialogue are likely more optimistic about the prospects for reducing the threat of terrorism.

TABLE 4 : CORRELATION : PERCENTAGE OF THOSE WHO AGREE WITH VARIOUS WAYS TO FIGHT TERRORISM, AS SEEN BY THOSE WHO ARE WORRIED ABOUT TERRORISM

Best way to fight terrorism	Worried about terrorist activity in Canada
Better dialogue/ better communication/ tolerance between cultures/ different beliefs and religions	44%
Better education for everyone (in the world)/ to fight ignorance	47%
Stricter immigration policies/ make the immigrants respect our laws/ our culture	65%
Security measures/ stricter laws/ security at borders (including passports)	75%
By punishing them/ an eye for an eye	75%

Source : ACS-Leger Marketing, March 2013

Despite the strong endorsement of interfaith dialogue as an antidote to terrorism, Charts 35 and 36 demonstrate that a majority of Canadians support the view that military force is the only possible recourse when it comes to dealing with state terrorism. The belief in dialogue on the domestic front does not therefore diminish the need for hard forceful action in addressing terrorism abroad.

CHART 35 : EXTENT TO WHICH CANADIANS AGREE THAT MILITARY STRENGTH IS THE ONLY WAY TO DEAL WITH THE THREAT OF STATE TERRORISM

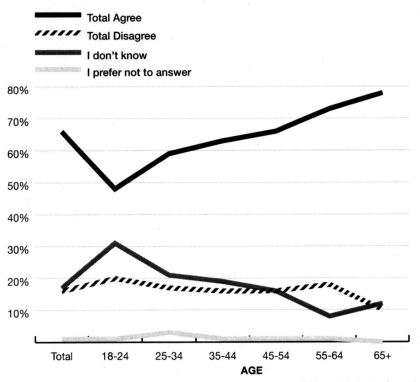

Source : ACS-Leger Marketing, September 2014

CHART 36 : EXTENT TO WHICH CANADIANS AGREE WITH THE GOVERNMENT OF CANADA'S MILITARY OPERATION (I.E., AIR STRIKES) AGAINST THE " ISLAMIC STATE (ISIS-ISIL) " IN IRAQ

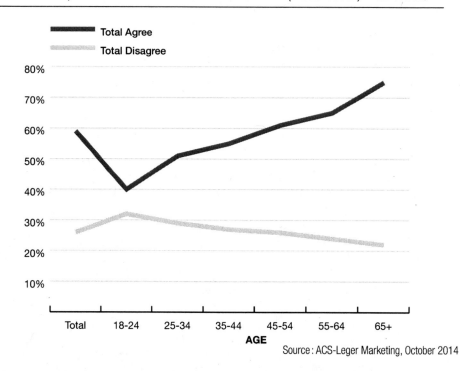

Source : ACS-Leger Marketing, October 2014

Although Canadians agree that military strength is the only way to deal with the threat of state terrorism, they are quite apprehensive about what to do in the event that a Canadian is held hostage by a terrorist group, as Chart 37 shows. Under such circumstances, there is considerable support for the idea that concessions be made to terrorists in working out a deal for release. In effect, Canadians are divided over the idea that there can be no negotiation with terrorists. Younger Canadians are particularly open to making such concessions in the event a Canadian were to be held hostage, with a slight majority of those between the ages of 18 and 24 supporting this view.

CHART 37 : EXTENT TO WHICH CANADIANS AGREE THAT WHEN A CANADIAN IS HELD HOSTAGE BY A TERRORIST GROUP, THE GOVERNMENT SHOULD WORK OUT A DEAL FOR HIS / HER RELEASE EVEN IF IT MEANS SOME CONCESSIONS TO TERRORISTS

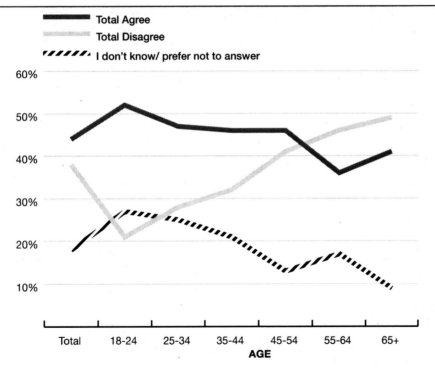

Source : ACS-Leger Marketing, September 2014

TERRORISM: WHO YA GONNA CALL?

To varying degrees and under diverging circumstances, Canadians may favour softer rather than harder approaches to counterterrorism. But one thing that garners rather significant support from Canadians is that intelligence services — to be specific, the Canadian Security and Intelligence Services (CSIS) — are best positioned to deal with the threat of terrorism. The paradox is that the work of CSIS has always been assumed to be highly confidential. Indeed, many may imagine CSIS as a group of persons that engage in clandestine intelligence gathering and may even wear those notorious trenchcoats. In fact, however, they have a website (*www.csis.gc.ca*), and the agency Director Michel Coulombe promises CSIS will fulfill its "mandate of keeping Canada and Canadians safe, but to do so in a way that is consistent with Canadian values" (Canadian Security and Intelligence Services, 2015, para. 15).

A majority of Canadians agree that CSIS is best positioned to address the threat of terrorism in the country. Some one in six Canadians believe that border security and immigration services are best positioned to do so, with one in eight selecting the military and the courts and justice system. Chart 38 reveals a caveat in the otherwise generalized preference for CSIS to meet the threat of terrorism, where Canadian Muslims are more divided in the way they respond to the question, with just above one-third selecting CSIS and over one in five choosing the courts and justice system. The difference may be attributable to the concern that Muslim Canadians are more often the target of intelligence work.

CHART 38 : RANKING OF WHICH INSTITUTIONS CANADIANS THINK ARE BEST POSITIONED TO ADDRESS THE THREAT OF TERRORISM

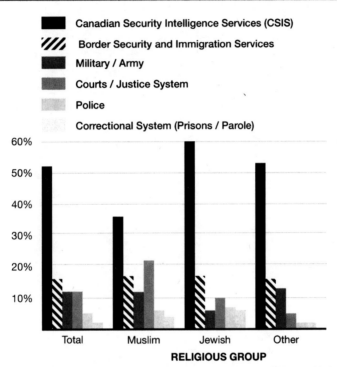

- Canadian Security Intelligence Services (CSIS)
- Border Security and Immigration Services
- Military / Army
- Courts / Justice System
- Police
- Correctional System (Prisons / Parole)

RELIGIOUS GROUP

Source : ACS-Leger Marketing, January 2014

If Canadians regard CSIS as best positioned to address the threat of terrorism, it is — thankfully — not the institution most would turn to in the event of a terrorist threat. As shown in Chart 39, the largest plurality of citizens would turn to the police, as would a majority of the country's ethnic minorities (defined in the survey as persons whose language spoken at home is neither English nor French). The military is the alternative for approximately one in seven Canadians.

CHART 39 : INSTITUTION THAT CANADIANS WOULD TURN TO FIRST IN THE EVENT OF A TERRORIST THREAT

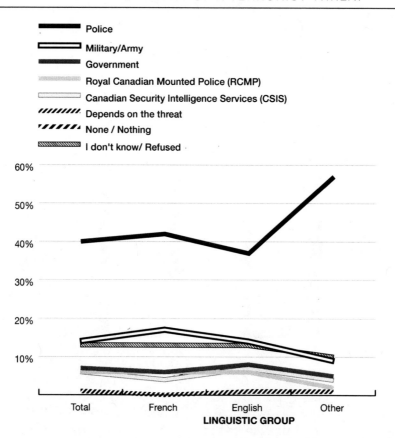

Legend:
- Police
- Military/Army
- Government
- Royal Canadian Mounted Police (RCMP)
- Canadian Security Intelligence Services (CSIS)
- Depends on the threat
- None / Nothing
- I don't know/ Refused

LINGUISTIC GROUP

Source : ACS-Leger Marketing, January 2014

It is worth noting with Chart 40 that the majority of Canadians hold a positive view of both the police and the military.

CHART 40 : EXTENT TO WHICH CANADIANS HOLD A POSITIVE VIEW OF THE POLICE AND MILITARY

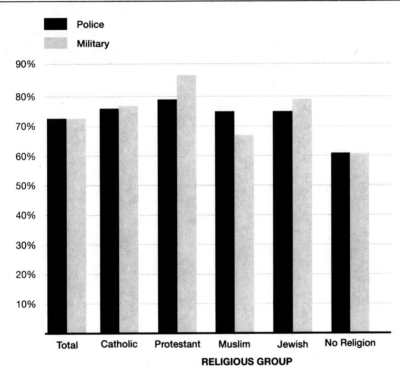

Source: ACS-Leger Marketing, March 2013

NATIONAL SECURITY AND GOVERNANCE

Matthew Waxman (2012) contends that it is natural to think of national security as primarily, if not exclusively, a centralized federal responsibility. That is, security is in the hands of federal defence and security departments and agencies. Federal jurisdiction over foreign affairs and defence also suggests primacy in the central government's protection of national security.

Chart 41 indicates that nearly two-thirds of Canadians agree that the federal government is better positioned than any other level of government to address the threat of terrorism.

JACK JEDWAB

CHART 41: EXTENT TO WHICH CANADIANS AGREE THAT THE FEDERAL GOVERNMENT IS BETTER POSITIONED THAN OTHER LEVELS OF GOVERNMENT TO ADDRESS THE THREAT OF TERRORISM IN CANADA

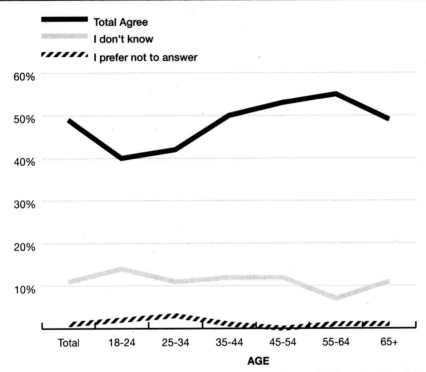

Source: ACS-Leger Marketing, October 2014

Effective counterterrorism is crucial to the government in maintaining public confidence in relevant decision-making and choosing certain strategies to address the threat of terrorism. Chart 42 indicates that less than one-third of Canadians believe that the threat of terrorism is being exaggerated by either the Canadian government or the Canadian media. Canadians under 35 years

81

of age are more likely than those over 35 to believe that the media is exaggerating the threat of terrorism more than the government.

CHART 42 : EXTENT TO WHICH CANADIANS AGREE THAT THE THREAT OF TERRORISM IS BEING EXAGGERATED BY THE GOVERNMENT OF CANADA OR THE CANADIAN MEDIA

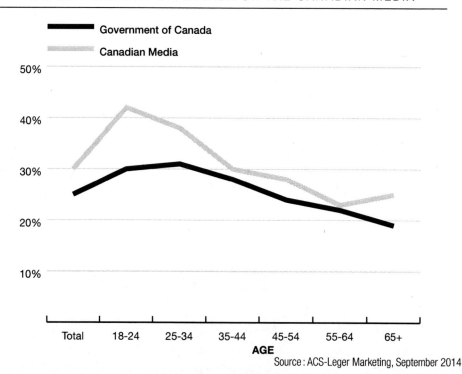

Source : ACS-Leger Marketing, September 2014

While the majority of Canadians do not think that the federal government is exaggerating the threat of terrorism, those who do not believe that the federal government is best positioned to address the threat feel otherwise, as shown in Chart 43. This finding illustrates the importance of maintaining public confidence in actions taken by the federal government to combat terrorism.

CHART 43 : CORRELATION : PERCENTAGE OF THOSE WHO AGREE THAT THE GOVERNMENT OF CANADA EXAGGERATES THE THREAT OF TERRORISM TO CANADIANS, AS SEEN BY THOSE AGREEING THAT THE FEDERAL GOVERNMENT IS BETTER POSITIONED THAN OTHER LEVELS OF GOVERNMENT TO ADDRESS THE THREAT OF TERRORISM

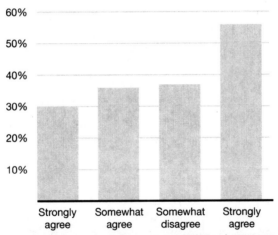

THE FEDERAL GOVERNMENT IS BETTER POSITIONED THAN OTHER LEVELS OF GOVERNMENT TO ADDRESS THE THREAT OF TERRORISM

Source : ACS-Leger Marketing, September 2014

What is the responsibility of the government with regard to conveying information to the public when it believes that there is a heightened risk of a terrorist attack? How is the public supposed to react to a higher alert? There is no simple answer. Bergin and Murphy (2015) argue that "it's no easy task for our political leaders to find language that conveys the need to be alert, while also creating a sense of calm" (para. 4). When the alert level is raised, the public may not know how to respond. The ultimate value of a public alert is to provide a threat assessment at a particular time and in doing so increase the number of eyes and ears in support of security and law enforcement agencies. If, however, nothing changes in the aftermath of a heightened alert, there is a risk that the public will become complacent and less vigilant the next time a heightened alert is issued.

The key question that arises from the challenge associated with security alerts may be the one posed earlier in this chapter. What and how much should the public know about counterterrorism? Sending out an alert without meaningful disclosure about the reasons for it will inevitably give rise to speculation and heighten anxiety (the latter isn't necessarily bad). Yet another issue is how much the public actually wants to know about counterterrorism. The fact that Canadians feel intelligence is the best way to address terrorism reveals that there is a certain understanding that discretion is often required in dealing with national security.

Our surveys reveal that more than half of Canadians agree that the Government of Canada should prohibit news media from releasing information about strategies to address terrorism. That sentiment is held quite similarly across the age spectrum and amongst all groups identifying by religion. Chart 44 shows that some two in three Canadians who agree that the government's counter-terrorism efforts are effective also support such a ban. And as revealed in the next table, it is Canadians that are most concerned about terrorist activity that favour such a ban.

CHART 44 : CORRELATION : PERCENTAGE OF THOSE WHO AGREE WITH PROHIBITING NEWS MEDIA FROM RELEASING INFORMATION ABOUT STRATEGIES TO ADDRESS TERRORISM, AS SEEN BY THE LEVEL OF WORRY ABOUT TERRORIST ACTIVITIES IN CANADA

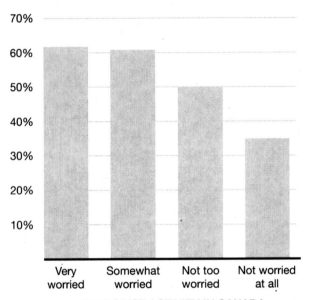

TERRORIST ACTIVITY IN CANADA

Source : ACS-Leger Marketing, September 2014

While the federal government is best positioned to take the lead when it comes to the fight against terrorism, cooperation with other levels of government is yet another essential element in effective counterterrorism. Federal, provincial, and municipal authorities share certain responsibilities when it comes to responding to terrorist threats. Provincial governments do policing as do municipal governments, which also have fire departments and emergency medical personnel that are typically first responders in the event of an incident.

Cross-governmental collaboration is vital since threats to national security can be diffused by considering available resources at all levels. Policymakers must develop strategies with a good grasp of the interests, capacity, and challenges across governments. While Canadians feel that the federal government should take the lead in counterterrorism, there has been pressure on all levels of government to demonstrate that they are taking action.

And the pressure has been mounting. In light of reports that about ten young Quebecers have been recruited to join Syrian jihadists, Montreal Mayor Denis Coderre announced the creation of an anti-radicalization centre. This softer counterterrorism initiative aims to strike a balance between "openness and vigilance" while providing assistance to families, friends, community organizations, and police (CBC News, March 10, 2015). The first of its kind in Montreal, the centre will involve partners from various sectors, including health and social services, public safety, and education. There has been a cautious response by some leaders of the Quebec Muslim community, claiming that were not properly consulted in this initiative.

ENGAGING CANADIANS TO SAY SOMETHING WHEN THEY SEE SOMETHING

Across the nation, we're all part of communities. In cities, on farms, and in the suburbs, we share everyday moments with our neighbors, colleagues, family, and friends. It's easy to take for granted the routine moments in our every day — going to work or school, the grocery store, or the gas station. But your everyday is different than your neighbor's — filled with the moments that make it uniquely yours. So if you see something you know shouldn't be there — or someone's behavior that doesn't seem quite right — say something. Because only you know what's supposed to be in your everyday.

Informed, alert communities play a critical role in keeping our nation safe. "If You See Something, Say Something™" engages the public in protecting our homeland through awareness–building, partnerships, and other outreach (Homeland Security, 2015).

The above provides the rationale for the United States Department of Homeland Security's program *If You See Something, Say Something*. Democratic governments committed to the fight against terrorism have become increasingly interested in engaging communities and citizens in the process, frequently reminding the population that security is a collective responsibility and we all have a role to play (although some of us clearly more so than others).

The Homeland Security campaign has not been without its critics. While it might be seen as a form of democratization of counterterrorism and a boost for civic engagement, some worry that it creates ambiguity in the relationship between citizen, officer, and suspect and may embolden some citizens into thinking they offer an extension to the government's policing imperatives.

A 2012 report issued by the United States Federal Emergency Management Agency (FEMA) points out that "residents know their communities best and are often the first to notice when something out of the ordinary occurs" (p. 2). Reduced resources and increased demands on law enforcement make for growing reliance on community members to offer accurate, reliable, and timely information regarding suspicious activities that may be indicators of terrorism.

This report reveals that community members are most aware of what is out of place, particularly in their own neighbourhoods, and they want to assist law enforcement in keeping their communities safe. When asked about motivators for reporting suspicious activity, 77 percent of Americans answered that they would report if they felt the activity could lead to harm to the community, and 74 percent of respondents stated that they would report if they believed the information would be useful to law enforcement.

How would Canadian citizens react when confronted with suspicious behaviour? Awareness of suspicious activity may emerge via interpersonal networks, and in that regard there may be personal knowledge of an individual or group who are considering something that constitutes a threat to public safety. In an attempt to probe the issue further, as seen in Chart 45, Canadians were asked whether they would report on someone they knew personally that they suspected of being engaged in criminal activity. The results have pointed to no meaningful difference across groups either on the basis of age or religious identification, with some 80 percent in agreement that they would do so.

CHART 45 : EXTENT TO WHICH CANADIANS AGREE THAT THEY WOULD REPORT SOMEONE THEY PERSONALLY KNEW TO THE POLICE IF HE OR SHE WERE INVOLVED IN A RADICALIZED ORGANIZATION

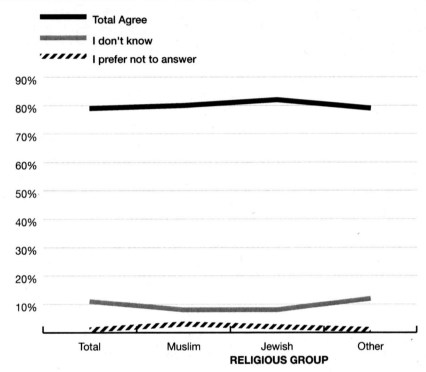

Source : ACS-Leger Marketing, January 2014

When looking at the relationship between the intention to report on someone involved in a radical organization and the perceived justification for terrorism in Chart 46, one observes that higher levels of agreement with the former proposition correlate with a greater tendency to reject any justification for terrorism.

CHART 46 : CORRELATION : PERCENTAGE OF THOSE WHO
STRONGLY AGREE THAT THERE IS NO JUSTIFICATION FOR
ACTS OF TERRORISM, AS SEEN BY THOSE AGREEING THAT IF
THEY KNEW SOMEONE PERSONALLY WHO IS INVOLVED IN A
RADICALIZED ORGANIZATION (CRIMINAL, VIOLENT, TERRORIST),
THEY WOULD REPORT HIM OR HER TO THE POLICE

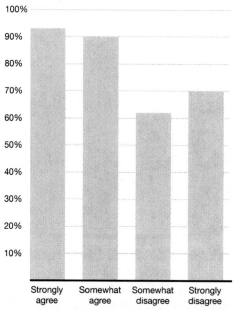

**IF I KNEW SOMEONE PERSONALLY WHO IS INVOLVED
IN A RADICALIZED ORGANIZATION (CRIMINAL, VIOLENT,
TERRORIST), I WOULD REPORT HIM OR HER TO THE POLICE**

Source : ACS-Leger Marketing, January 2014

As government seeks to enlist citizens in the process of reporting suspicious
activity, it elevates the level of collective responsibility in addressing threats to

public safety. We observed that Canadians are willing to report on the suspicious activity of someone with whom they have personal contact. Should Canadians in any way feel responsible for egregious acts committed by someone from a community with which they identify? Ideally they should not feel any such responsibility unless they have somehow influenced someone in pursuing such a course of action. Yet as seen in Chart 47, a relatively important percentage of Canadians (more than one-third) report feeling some responsibility when a racist act is committed by someone from the community with which they identify. Moreover, a majority of Canadians feel they should publicly denounce someone from the same community who commits a racially motivated crime.

CHART 47 : EXTENT TO WHICH CANADIANS FEEL RESPONSIBLE FOR EGREGIOUS ACTS COMMITTED BY SOMEONE FROM THEIR COMMUNITY

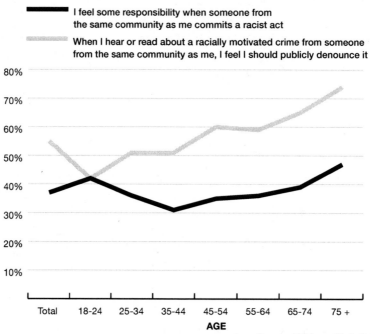

I feel some responsibility when someone from the same community as me commits a racist act

When I hear or read about a racially motivated crime from someone from the same community as me, I feel I should publicly denounce it

Source : ACS-Leger Marketing, March 2015

Not surprisingly, Chart 48 demonstrates that the more you feel compelled to publicly denounce someone from the same community who has committed a racially motivated crime, the more vehement you are about the obligation to report "radicalized" individuals to the police. Hence, some may feel that raising the level of communal responsibility for acts committed by fellow community members will bring about positive outcomes in the fight against extremism, but such a generalization risks stigmatizing community members with potentially counterproductive results.

CHART 48 : CORRELATION : PERCENTAGE OF THOSE WHO STRONGLY AGREE THAT IF THEY KNEW SOMEONE PERSONALLY INVOLVED IN A RADICALIZED ORGANIZATION, THEY WOULD REPORT HIM OR HER TO THE POLICE, AS SEEN BY THOSE FEELING THEY SHOULD PUBLICLY DENOUNCE A RACIALLY MOTIVATED CRIME FROM SOMEONE FROM THE SAME COMMUNITY AS THEM

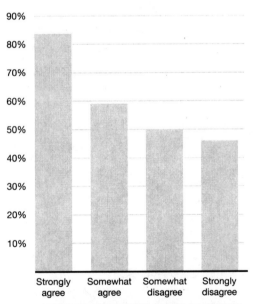

WHEN I HEAR OR READ ABOUT A RACIALLY MOTIVATED CRIME FROM SOMEONE FROM THE SAME COMMUNITY AS ME, I FEEL I SHOULD PUBLICLY DENOUNCE IT

Source : ACS-Leger Marketing, March 2015

Engaging individuals in the process of counterterrorism appears less complicated than engaging communities. This is especially true when members of the community feel that they are the object of particular scrutiny. As noted earlier, we are increasingly reminded that security is a collective responsibility in which individuals and communities have a role to play. However, some groups are perceived to have more responsibility than others, and many members feel this way too.

In a report entitled *Bringing it Home* (2006), the British-based think tank Demos stresses the need for putting communities at the heart of approaches to counterterrorism. Advocating a community based approach to counterterrorism, Demos emphasizes social justice and community cohesion by tackling poverty, low educational attainment, and discrimination against Muslims. The report points out that communities which feel deprived, victimized, or threatened will likely generate individuals that express their frustrations in a variety of ways. Demos researchers Briggs, Fieschi, and Lownsbrough provide four reasons in support of a community-based approach working alongside the Muslim population:

1. the communities offer important sources of information and intelligence: our own in-built early warning system;
2. the communities picking up these signs are best placed to act pre-emptively to divert their young people from extremism: the self-policing society;
3. while the state must also play a role, communities must take the lead in tackling problems that either create grievances or hinder their ability to organize, such as poverty, poor educational and employment attainment, and the paucity of effective leadership and representation; and
4. the police and security service cannot act without the consent of the communities they are there to protect.

Briggs, Fieschi, and Lownsbrough add that a community based approach to counterterrorism must be underpinned by four principles:

1. it must be locally based and recognize and respond to the differences within the Muslim community, which is far from homogenous;

2. it needs to be rooted in an understanding of faith, without which it is easy for government and security forces to misread the signs within the community;

3. the government must make the policymaking process as transparent and accountable as possible, opening up decision-making processes and engaging on issues where there is political discontent. Only then will trust be forged between the government and Muslim communities; and

4. the government must get over its hang-ups about responding to the grievances of the Muslim community.

In the next chapter, we will consider the challenges associated with pursuing some of these proposals as they bear upon the relationship between counterterrorism and identities. We'll reflect upon whether the community-based approach needs to consider broader societal attitudes and pressures in addressing relations between communities and upon the way that broader public views may constrain strategy and practice in countering terrorism.

CHAPTER 5

SECURITY, IDENTITY, AND RELIGIOUS PLURALISM

Discussion of counterterrorism in conjunction with identities can be particularly toxic for persons identifying as Muslim. When the threat of terrorism is evoked in a conversation about religion, Islam often comes to mind. These days, the expression of concern about religious minorities, religious diversity, or religious pluralism is almost always a euphemism for anxieties about Muslims. As we will observe, the expression of concern about non-Christian immigrants also tends to be a cover for anxieties about Muslims.

ISLAM AND SECURITY

In 2013-2014, debates within Quebec over the adoption of the Charter of Values (which proposed a ban on religious symbols in the civil service) offered a classic example of discourse around the worrisome role of religion as a front for widespread anxiety about the purported rise in the domestic influence of the Islamic faith.

Although on a lesser scale, the Quebec debate over the Charter of Values resonated with other Canadians. As illustrated in Chart 49, those who regard religious pluralism as a liability are far more likely to hold negative views of Muslims than those with positive views of pluralism. Similarly, in Chart 50, those who see religion as divisive are more likely to hold negative views of Muslims and far more likely to have an unfavourable view of relations between Muslims and non-Muslims.

CHART 49 : CORRELATION : PERCENTAGE OF THOSE WHO HAVE A NEGATIVE PERCEPTION OF MUSLIMS AND OF MUSLIM-NON-MUSLIM RELATIONS, AS SEEN BY THOSE WHO AGREE OR DISAGREE THAT HAVING MANY RELIGIOUS GROUPS IS MORE A LIABILITY THAN AN ASSET

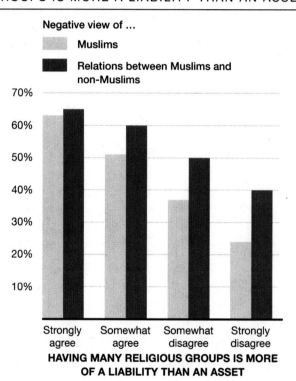

Negative view of ...

Muslims

Relations between Muslims and non-Muslims

HAVING MANY RELIGIOUS GROUPS IS MORE OF A LIABILITY THAN AN ASSET

Source : ACS-Leger Marketing, March 2013

CHART 50 : CORRELATION : PERCENTAGE OF THOSE WHO HAVE A NEGATIVE PERCEPTION OF MUSLIMS AND OF MUSLIM-NON-MUSLIM RELATIONS, AS SEEN BY THOSE WHO AGREE OR DISAGREE THAT RELIGION BRINGS PEOPLE TOGETHER MORE THAN IT DIVIDES THEM

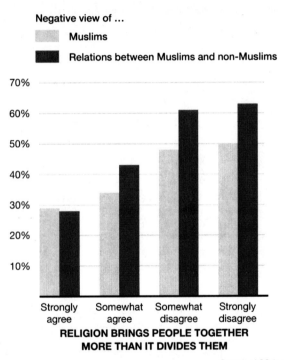

Source : ACS-Leger Marketing, March 2013

In 1993, the late Samuel Huntington published his highly controversial essay entitled *The Clash of Civilizations ?* in ***Foreign Affairs Magazine,*** which he then expanded upon in the 1996 book entitled *The Clash of Civilizations and the Remaking of World Order*. Huntington argues against the notion of a universal civilization, stating that human beings are divided along cultural lines — Western, Islamic, Hindu, and so on — with their own distinct sets of values. According to Huntington, Islamic civilization is the most troublesome, given that Muslims' primary attachment is to their religion, not the nation-state, and that their culture is unreceptive to certain liberal ideals like pluralism, individualism, and democracy (Brooks, 2011). He traces this cultural clash back 1300 years and believes it to be even more engrained and polarizing due to the 1990 Gulf War (Huntington, 1996).

Less than five years after the release of his book, the events of 9/11 and the ensuing threat of terrorism popularized what became commonly referred to as the Huntington thesis. Based on the positions taken by non-Western civilizations to preserve religion and customs in a world that is increasingly influenced by secular Western philosophies, cultural differences among civilizations has been pushed to the forefront of world politics (Douglas and Wentz, n.d.).

His critics contend that Huntington's arguments are a vast oversimplification as a whole, using broad concepts of language, history, customs, institutions, and most importantly religion. His ambiguity in the use of these terms demonstrates a disconnect between his theoretical argument and the cultural reality of the world we live in today, for individuals involved in Islamic terrorist organizations constitute an extremist minority, which Huntington does not acknowledge (Flynn-Piercy, 2011). By undermining political and national self-interest, Huntington's claims are vague enough to actually appear accurate (Swan 2010).

The Canadian public thinks otherwise, siding with Huntington on the idea that there is a clash. (There is an important caveat which will be examined later in the chapter). As revealed in Chart 51, some eight surveys conducted between 2012 and 2015 consistently reveal that between 55 and 60 percent of Canadians subscribe to the Huntingdon thesis.

CHART 51 : EVOLUTION OF THE EXTENT TO WHICH CANADIANS AGREE THAT THERE IS AN IRRECONCILABLE CONFLICT BETWEEN THE WEST AND MUSLIMS

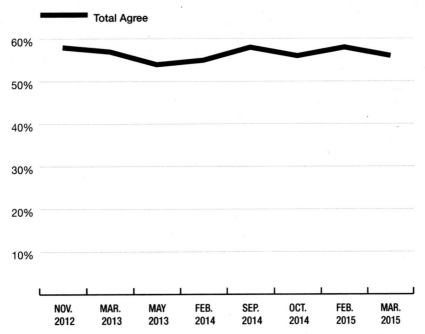

Source : ACS-Leger Marketing

With regard to the views of Canada's religious groups on the idea of a civilizational clash, Chart 52 indicates that Muslims are more likely to disagree than agree with the notion, but most non-Muslim Canadians feel differently. Approximately two-thirds of Catholics, Protestants, and Jews surveyed believe that the presumed conflict is irreconcilable.

CHART 52 : EXTENT TO WHICH CANADIAN RELIGIOUS GROUPS AGREE THAT THERE IS AN IRRECONCILABLE CONFLICT BETWEEN WESTERN SOCIETIES AND MUSLIM SOCIETIES

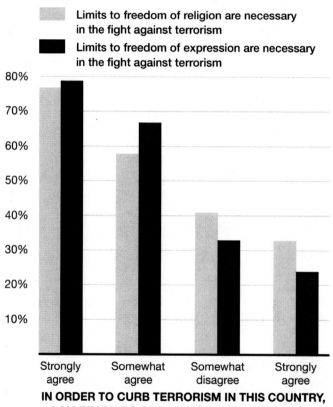

Limits to freedom of religion are necessary in the fight against terrorism

Limits to freedom of expression are necessary in the fight against terrorism

IN ORDER TO CURB TERRORISM IN THIS COUNTRY, I AM READY TO GIVE UP SOME CIVIL LIBERTIES

Source : ACS-Leger Marketing, March 2013

HOW 9/11 POPULARIZED
THE HUNTINGTON THESIS

Earlier we pointed to the events of 9/11 having a lingering effect on the contemporary level of anxiety about terrorism. Canadians also acknowledge that 9/11 has significantly modified views on relations between religious groups in Canada, as seen in Chart 53. Francophone Canadians are the most likely to admit such an impact, while Canadian Muslims are least likely to feel that their views on such relations have been altered as a consequence of 9/11.

CHART 53 : EXTENT TO WHICH CANADIANS AGREE THAT THE EVENTS OF SEPTEMBER 11, 2001, HAVE CHANGED THEIR VIEW OF RELATIONS BETWEEN RELIGIOUS GROUPS IN CANADA

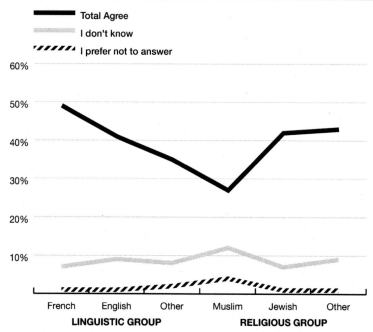

Source : ACS-Leger Marketing, January 2014

An illustration of how Canadians, who describe themselves as particularly marked by the events of 9/11, view Muslims is offered in Table 5. We can see considerable differences between those whose views have purportedly been most affected and those least so on the clash of civilizations, around the perceived threat of non-Christian immigrants, with regard to concerns over relations between Muslims and non-Muslims, and in terms of negative views and trust Muslims.

JACK JEDWAB

TABLE 5 : CORRELATION : VIEWS ON SELECTED ISSUES, AS SEEN
BY THOSE WHO STRONGLY AGREE OR STRONGLY DISAGREE THAT
EVENTS OF SEPTEMBER 11, 2001, HAVE CHANGED THEIR VIEW
OF RELATIONS BETWEEN RELIGIOUS GROUPS IN CANADA

Agreement: The events of september 11, 2011 have changed my views of relations between religious groups in canada	Strongly agree	Strongly disagree
There is an irreconcilable conflict between Western societies and Muslim societies	84%	35%
Society is threatened by the influx of non-Christian immigrants to Canada	70%	22%
Concerned over relations between Muslims and non-Muslims	75%	43%
Negative view of Muslims	69%	23%
Trust Muslims in Canada	22%	65%

Source : ACS-Leger Marketing, January 2014

   Looking overall at the perceived state of relations between communities, it is observed in Chart 54 that the relationship which concerns Canadians the most is between Muslims and non-Muslims. Canadians are more concerned about relations between Muslims and non-Muslims than about those between Muslims and Jews. Canadian Jews have reported the highest concern in relations between Muslims and Jews. Although many express concern, Muslims are far less concerned than Jews with the relationship between Muslims and Jews. Overall, there is considerably less concern amongst Canadians about the relationship between Jews and non-Jews than there is between Muslims and non-Muslims and Muslims and Jews (although that perception is not shared by Canada's Jews).

CHART 54 : TOTAL CONCERN OF CANADIANS IN TERMS
OF RELATIONS BETWEEN SELECTED GROUPS

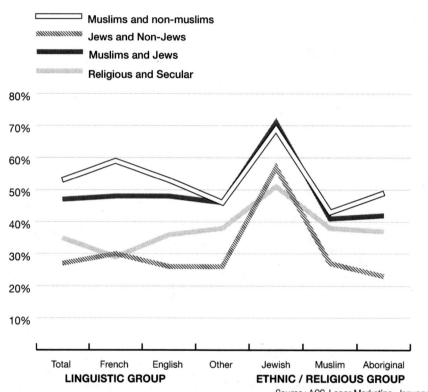

Legend:
- Muslims and non-muslims
- Jews and Non-Jews
- Muslims and Jews
- Religious and Secular

LINGUISTIC GROUP: Total, French, English, Other
ETHNIC / RELIGIOUS GROUP: Jewish, Muslim, Aboriginal

Source : ACS-Leger Marketing, January 2014

It has been suggested that perceived tensions between Muslims and non-Muslims and Jews and non-Jews are merely a reflection of concerns about the impact of religious expression on secularism and hence that negative responses on these questions are a function of secularist preference for greater separation of Church from state. Without denying that this may very partially explain expressed tensions around relations between religious groups, if it were accurate one might expect that similar levels of anxiety would be expressed about the religious and the secular. That, however, is not the case, as Chart 55 reveals considerably less concern over that relationship.

CHART 56 : EXTENT TO WHICH CANADIANS HAVE A POSITIVE
OPINION OF RELATIONS BETWEEN MUSLIMS AND JEWS,
MUSLIMS AND NON-MUSLIMS, AND RELIGIOUS AND SECULAR

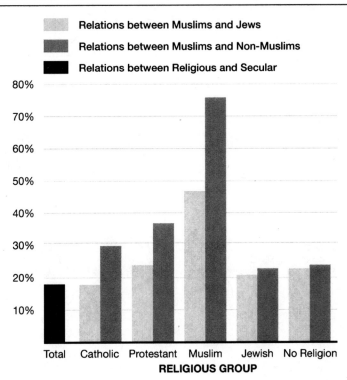

Source : ACS-Leger Marketing, March 2013

High levels of concern over relations between Muslims and non-Muslims or, for that matter, Jews and non-Jews, do not necessarily imply that such feelings are characterized by hostility towards the respective groups. Table 6 reveals that some 40 percent of those reporting they are somewhat concerned about the relations between Muslims and non-Muslims hold a favourable view of Muslims. However, some one in four Canadians that say they are very concerned over such relations hold a positive view of Muslims. In contrast, just under half of those Canadians expressing the highest concern over the relationship between Jews and non-Jews have a positive view of Jews.

TABLE 6 : CORRELATION : PERCENTAGE OF THOSE WHO HAVE POSITIVE VIEWS OF MUSLIMS AND JEWS, AS SEEN BY THOSE WITH VARIOUS LEVELS OF CONCERN ABOUT RELATIONS BETWEEN MUSLIMS AND NON-MUSLIMS

Positive view of	Level of concern over relations between Muslims and non-Muslims			
	Very converned	Somewhat concerned	Not very concerned	Not concerned at all
Muslims	27%	42%	56%	51%
	Level of concern over relations between Jews and non-Jews			
Jews	47%	68%	76%	72%

Source : ACS-Leger Marketing, March 2013

108

CANADIAN OPINIONS OF RELIGIOUS GROUPS

Negative opinions held about a particular group cannot be perfectly equated with racism. Indeed, it is possible for someone to not feel positive about a group without being racist. Still there remain good reasons to be concerned when someone says I am not a racist but I don't trust Muslims and/or Jews. The underlying generalizations implied by unfavourable views of identifiable groups are unhealthy for social solidarity in multicultural democracies like Canada.

With regard to Canadians' opinions of religious groups and atheists, Chart 56 demonstrates that Muslims elicit by far the lowest share of positive opinion overall. Opinion of Muslims is especially low amongst Francophones in Quebec. But against the ratings given to other groups, Muslims get low positives from all non-Francophones and Jews. For their part, Muslims hold a lower opinion of atheists/agnostics than they do of other groups. Muslims hold somewhat more favourable opinions of Jews than the inverse. Francophones hold a less favourable opinion of Jews than of Muslims.

CHART 56 : CANADIANS' POSITIVE OPINION OF SELECTED GROUPS

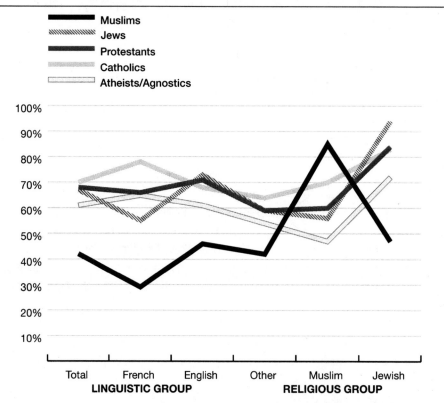

Source : ACS-Leger Marketing, January 2014

There is a definite correlation between the negative opinion of Muslims and anxiety about terrorism on the part of Canadians. Chart 57 indicates that some three in four Canadians who hold very negative views about Muslims are worried about terrorist activity in Canada, as are nearly two in three Canadians who hold somewhat negative views about Muslims.

CHART 57 : CORRELATION : PERCENTAGE OF THOSE WHO ARE WORRIED ABOUT TERRORIST ACTIVITY IN CANADA, ON THE BASIS OF POSITIVE OR NEGATIVE OPINIONS OF MUSLIMS

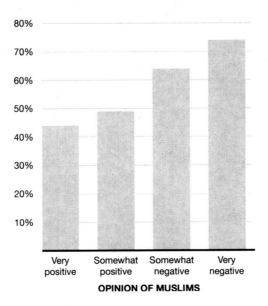

Source : ACS-Leger Marketing, January 2014

As seen in Chart 58, in the 2012-2014 period, there was a decrease in positive opinion about Muslims. While the negative trending is not easy to explain, it is likely connected to images conveyed to the public about the overseas and domestic threat of Islamic fundamentalism. Greater attention needs to be directed at how to reverse this trend, as such negative opinion risks contributing to greater feelings of exclusion amongst Muslims.

CHART 58 : EVOLUTION OF CANADIANS' POSITIVE OPINION OF MUSLIMS

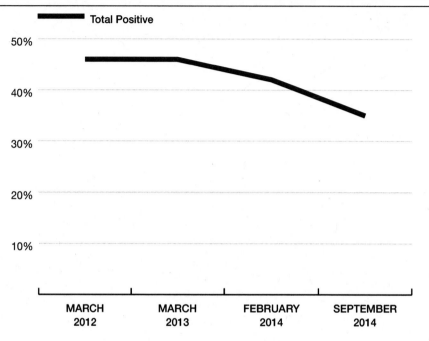

Source : ACS-Leger Marketing

In her book *Trust, Democracy and Multicultural Challenges*, Patti Lenard (2012) insists that "a central issue in cultural and ethnic tensions is trust relations or the absence of them amongst citizens" (p. 156). She argues that building trust is vital in multicultural democracies, adding that this is essential to reducing vulnerability in order to extend and reciprocate trust. Undoubtedly, feelings of anxiety and hostility contribute to undermining intergroup trust. Chart 59 illustrates the large gap in trust of Muslims between those harbouring very positive and very negative views of the group.

CHART 59 : CORRELATION : PERCENTAGE OF THOSE WHO TRUST MUSLIMS, AS SEEN BY THOSE WITH VERY POSITIVE OR VERY NEGATIVE OPINIONS ABOUT MUSLIMS

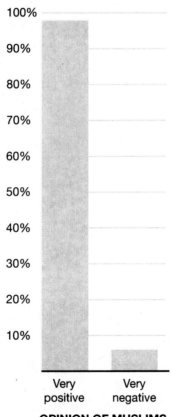

OPINION OF MUSLIMS

Source : ACS-Leger Marketing, March 2013

All is not dire. Overall, as seen in Chart 60, levels of trust remain fairly positive and, despite the strong negative opinion towards Muslims, some two in three Canadians report that they trust them a lot or somewhat. This represents somewhat less than the degree of trust extended to Catholics, Protestants, and Jews in Canada, but suggests potential for improving intergroup relations.

CHART 60 : EXTENT TO WHICH CANADIANS
TRUST VARIOUS RELIGIOUS GROUPS

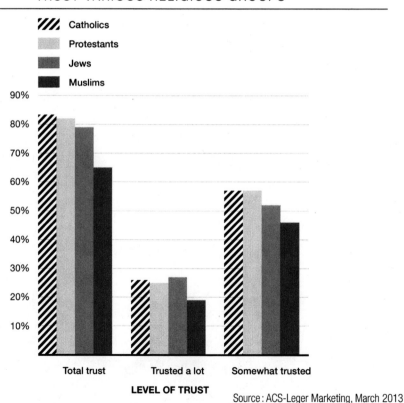

Source : ACS-Leger Marketing, March 2013

Yet another paradox is found in Chart 61 in the degree to which Canadians manifest concern about increasing anti-Muslim and anti-Jewish feelings. Despite the high level of negative sentiment towards Muslims, a majority of Canadians are concerned about rising anti-Muslim sentiment in Canada. A majority of Canada's Jews express such concern. Not surprisingly, both Jews and Muslims express higher levels of concern with rising anti-Semitism and rising anti-Muslim sentiment, respectively.

CHART 61 : CANADIANS WORRIED ABOUT THE RISE IN ANTI-MUSLIM SENTIMENT AND ANTI-SEMITISM IN CANADA

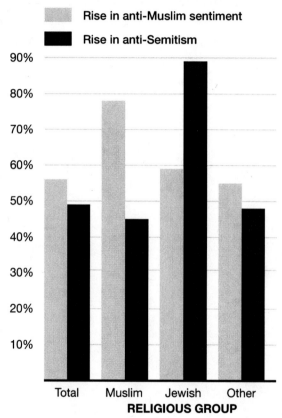

Source : ACS-Leger Marketing, January 2014

Chart 62 demonstrates that a majority of Canadians holding somewhat negative views of Muslims are worried about anti-Muslim sentiment, as are 40 percent of those harbouring negative views of Muslims.

CHART 62 : CORRELATION : PERCENTAGE OF THOSE WHO WORRY ABOUT THE RISE OF ANTI-MUSLIM SENTIMENT, AS SEEN BY THOSE WITH POSITIVE OR NEGATIVE OPINIONS ABOUT MUSLIMS

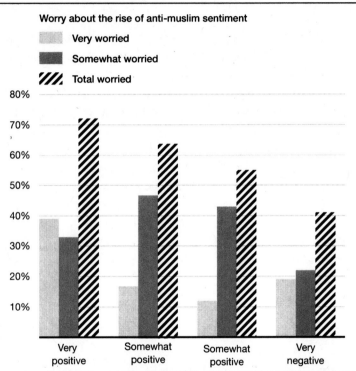

DO YOU HAVE A VERY POSITIVE, SOMEWHAT POSITIVE, SOMEWHAT NEGATIVE OR VERY NEGATIVE OPINION OF THE FOLLOWING GROUPS: MUSLIMS

Source : ACS-Leger Marketing, January 2014

COUNTERTERRORISM AND IDENTITIES : CANADIAN VIEWPOINTS

SENTIMENTS TOWARDS ISLAM AND MUSLIMS

We have been looking at the varying aspects of sentiment held towards Muslims, including trust of Muslims and the perceived state of relations between Muslims and non-Muslims. We have done so where relevant in contrast with other groups. But to what extent are distinctions made between the Islamic faith and the people who identify with it? Is it the negative sentiment directed at individuals that is driving antipathy towards the religion, is it animosity towards the religion spilling onto its followers, or are the two intertwined?

In what might be described as a word association test, in June 2010 Canadians were asked to respond positively or negatively to various terms. A majority of Canadians reacted favourably when they saw the term Religion, more so than Church, as seen in Chart 63. More Canadians reacted positively than they did negatively when seeing Catholicism, Protestantism, and Judaism. But there was considerably greater negative than positive reaction to the term Islam (Jedwab, 2010).

CHART 63 : CANADIAN RHETORIC TEST — RELIGION

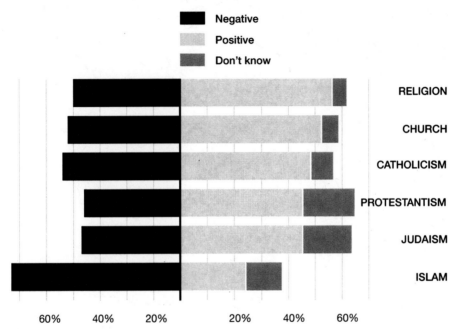

Source : Jedwab, 2010

It is likely that many Muslims attribute the high degree of negative sentiment directed at Islam to its portrayal in the public domain — mostly via domestic and international media. Indeed, Chart 64 demonstrates that a majority of Muslims agree that minority religions are misrepresented in Canada, more so than any other religious group.

CHART 64 : EXTENT TO WHICH CANADIANS AGREE THAT
MINORITY RELIGIONS ARE MISREPRESENTED IN CANADA

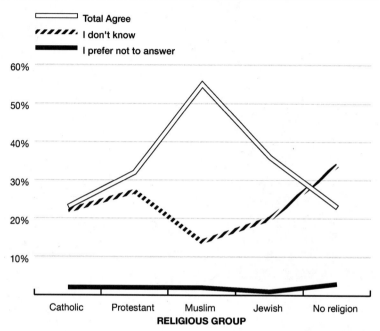

Source : ACS-Leger Marketing, March 2013

In *Managing Ethnic Diversity After 9/11*, Chebel and Reich (2010) point out that a majority of Westerners have little knowledge of Islam. A 2005 poll conducted in the United States showed that 60 percent of the population said they were not knowledgeable about Islam. They suggest that this situation favoured the spreading of negative stereotypes and propaganda against Muslims.

In Chart 65, when asked whether they possessed knowledge of the history of various religions, some two-thirds of Canadians say they are either very or somewhat knowledgeable about the history of Christianity. Knowledge about Islam is considerably lower, with one in four Canadians reporting being knowledgeable about its history. Some two in three also report not being knowledgeable about the history of Judaism.

CHART 65 : CANADIANS' KNOWLEDGE OF THE HISTORY
OF CHRISTIANITY, JUDAISM, AND ISLAM

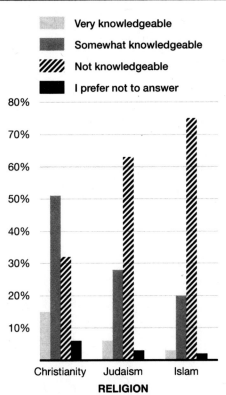

Very knowledgeable
Somewhat knowledgeable
Not knowledgeable
I prefer not to answer

Source : ACS-Leger Marketing, January 2014

While Canadians admit to having relatively low knowledge of non-Christian religions, Chart 66 indicates that a majority of persons identifying as Christians think they possess a good knowledge of of the cultural values and religious beliefs of some other cultures. A markedly higher share of Muslims and Jews reports good knowledge of the values and religious beliefs of others.

CHART 66 : CANADIANS AGREE THAT THEY HAVE A GOOD KNOWLEDGE OF THE CULTURAL VALUES AND RELIGIOUS BELIEFS OF SOME OTHER CULTURES

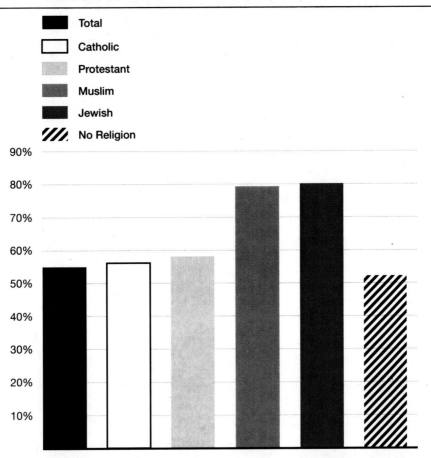

Source : ACS-Leger Marketing, March 2013

Higher knowledge begets higher interest, and hence our surveys reveal in Chart 67 that when asked whether they want to learn more about religions other than their own, the highest interest in doing so is expressed by Canadian Jews and Muslims. Protestants and Catholics express less interest in learning about other religions, and those identifying as having no religion are the least interested.

CHART 67 : EXTENT TO WHICH CANADIANS AGREE THAT THEY WANT TO LEARN MORE ABOUT RELIGIONS OTHER THAN THEIR OWN

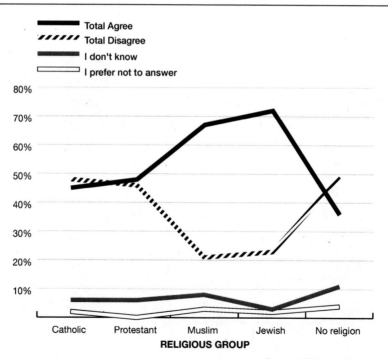

Source : ACS-Leger Marketing, March 2013

Advocates of multicultural or cross-cultural education insist that greater knowledge about religions and cultures will result in more openness. Undoubtedly, education helps in the process of demystification of cultures and religions, and even if it does not reap the benefit of enhancing tolerance on its own, the acquisition of such knowledge is good both for the individual and society.

It is an oversimplification, however, to assume that intolerance or indifference towards Muslims is largely a function of ignorance about Islam amongst non-Muslims. It would not be surprising to hear such views espoused by faith leaders who regularly express concerns about the lack of knowledge on the part of non-members as well as members of their own faiths. It is part of the educational mission of the clergy to never be satisfied about the level of knowledge about their particular faith.

Regrettably, our surveys provide relatively little support for the idea that greater knowledge of minority religions will either undercut certain key generalizations or ease anxiety with respect to terrorism. As Table 7 shows, at best such knowledge provides a decline in negative sentiments towards Muslims amongst some groups.

TABLE 7 : CORRELATION : VIEWS ON IRRECONCILABLE CONFLICT AND
OPINION ABOUT MUSLIMS, AS SEEN BY SELECTED RELIGIOUS GROUPS
ON THE BASIS OF REPORTING GOOD OR POOR KNOWLEDGE OF THE
CULTURAL VALUES AND RELIGIOUS BELIEFS OF OTHER CULTURES

Agreement: I have a good knowledge of the cultural values and religious beliefs of some other cultures						
	Catholics		Protestants		Jews	
	Good knowledge	Poor knowledge	Good knowledge	Poor knowledge	Good knowledge	Poor knowledge
There is an irreconcilable conflict between Western societies and Muslim societies	68%	62%	56%	73%	60%	60%
Worry about terrorist activity	68%	68%	58%	62%	66%	63%
Positive views of Muslims	40%	33%	62%	33%	55%	60%

Source : ACS-Leger Marketing, March 2013

If greater knowledge of Islam on the part of non-Muslims is not the panacea that will fundamentally alter the state of relations between Muslims and non-Muslims and build trust in Muslims, then what might contribute to doing so? Our surveys suggest that one important avenue lies in greater interaction or personal contact with Muslims. More contact with members of specific cultural and religious groups results in more favourable perceptions of the associated group. Chart 68 offers a very clear illustration of the positive outcome arising from the degree of frequency of contact with Muslims.

CHART 68 : CORRELATION : OPINIONS OF MUSLIMS FOR CANADIANS, BASED ON THEIR REPORTED DEGREE OF CONTACT WITH MUSLIMS

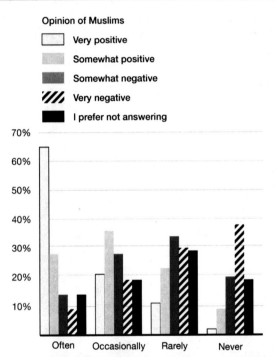

Opinion of Muslims
- Very positive
- Somewhat positive
- Somewhat negative
- Very negative
- I prefer not answering

IN THE LAST PAST YEAR, HAVE YOU OFTEN, OCCASIONALLY, RARELY OR NEVER HAD CONTACT WITH MUSLIMS

Source : ACS-Leger Marketing, March 2013

Our survey reveals in Chart 69 that Jews report the highest levels of contact with Muslims relative to other religious groups surveyed here. Catholics have the lowest degree of contact and, as revealed earlier, hold the highest degree of negative sentiment towards Muslims.

CHART 69 : EXTENT TO WHICH CANADIAN RELIGIOUS
GROUPS HAVE CONTACT WITH MUSLIMS AND JEWS

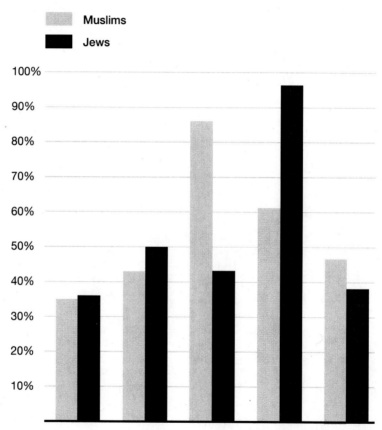

Source : ACS-Leger Marketing, March 2013

Yet another example of the benefits of contact with Muslims is the higher level
of trust associated with the frequency of the contact as observed in Chart 70.

CHART 70 : CORRELATION : PERCENTAGE OF TRUST IN MUSLIMS FOR CANADIANS, BASED ON THEIR REPORTED DEGREE OF CONTACT WITH MUSLIMS

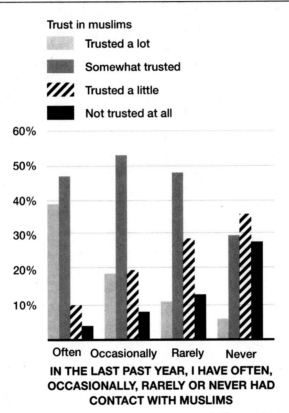

Trust in muslims

Trusted a lot

Somewhat trusted

Trusted a little

Not trusted at all

IN THE LAST PAST YEAR, I HAVE OFTEN, OCCASIONALLY, RARELY OR NEVER HAD CONTACT WITH MUSLIMS

Source : ACS-Leger Marketing, March 2013

RECONCILABLE IRRECONCILABILITY?

It was suggested at the beginning of this chapter that there was a caveat in Canadians' endorsement of the Huntington thesis. In effect, while a majority of Canadians agree with Huntington's proposition, a majority also believe that interfaith dialogue is essential in combating the threat of terrorism. Contradictory as this may seem, Chart 71 demonstrates that seven in ten of those most convinced that we are facing irreconcilable conflict believe in dialogue as a critical counterterrorism measure. There is hope. Based on the empirical evidence presented above, we submit that it is not the theological dialogue but rather the contact between persons of different communities to which dialogue gives rise that offers the possibility for reconciliation.

CHART 71 : CORRELATION : PERCENTAGE OF THOSE WHO AGREE THAT DIALOGUE BETWEEN RELIGIOUS OFFICIALS IS ESSENTIAL IN COMBATING THE THREAT OF TERRORISM, AS SEEN BY THOSE THAT AGREE OR DISAGREE THAT THERE IS AN IRRECONCILABLE CONFLICT BETWEEN WESTERN SOCIETIES AND ISLAMIC TEXT AND PRACTICES IN THE WORLD

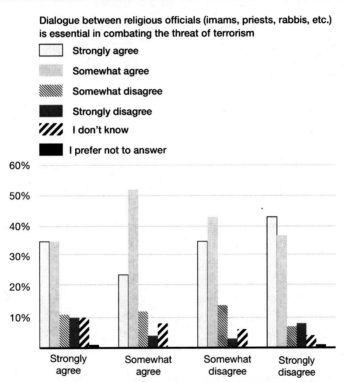

Dialogue between religious officials (imams, priests, rabbis, etc.) is essential in combating the threat of terrorism

- Strongly agree
- Somewhat agree
- Somewhat disagree
- Strongly disagree
- I don't know
- I prefer not to answer

THERE IS AN IRRECONCILABLE CONFLICT BETWEEN WESTERN SOCIETIES AND ISLAMIC TEXT AND PRACTICES IN THE WORLD

Source : ACS-Leger Marketing, March 2015

At the end of Chapter 4, we referred to the proposals of the British think tank Demos, which recommended community policing in areas with a high population of Muslims as an essential element in counterterrorism. The proposed community-based strategy would have a more knowledgeable police force, approaching the community with a better rooted understanding of faith. This would empower the community to enable effective policing and avoid polarizing them. However, this bilateralism does not tackle the broader challenge of diminishing generalizations and stereotypes about members of Muslim communities. Demos further suggests an approach that seeks to reduce social injustice, providing a direct benefit to counterterrorism (Briggs, Fieschi, and Lownsbrough, 2006).

Chebel and Reich (2010) insist that too often counterterrorism measures have resulted in an increasing sense of alienation in the very minorities whose cooperation is essential. The result has sometimes heightened feelings of discrimination against Muslims and, ironically, a greater sense of vulnerability.

It would be wrong to argue that the singular explanation for the radicalization of Muslims is attributable to perceived intolerance of the Islamic faith. But there is no question that discrimination and racism in society are contributing factors to the conditions that foster radicalization. Hence there is no underestimating the need for societal commitment to combating racism and prejudice as a key element in medium and long term strategies to combat terrorism. This commitment needs to be accompanied by a renewed resolve to protect civil liberties.

Too often these important considerations are lost in the articulation of strategies to combat terrorism. The next chapter will focus on the ongoing debate regarding the protection of civil liberties and its presumed impact on the effectiveness of counterterrorism.

JACK JEDWAB

MODELS OF DIVERSITY AND COUNTERTERRORISM: THE "OVER-THE-COUNTER" NARRATIVE

Since the beginning of the twenty-first century, debates over the place of minority religions in Canada have moved to the centre of several policy discussions, notably with regard to the challenges associated with multiculturalism. Some observers have suggested that terrorist attacks in Canada and elsewhere should encourage the rethinking of multiculturalism policies. They suggest that multiculturalism results in the active promotion of group traditions at the expense of integration and thus creates environments that enable the propagation of undemocratic views. Incidents of terrorism have contributed to pronouncements of the death of multiculturalism by European politicians. However, proponents of multiculturalism believe that it is fundamentalism that looks unfavourably upon pluralism and the accommodation of difference.

Debates over models of diversity have increasingly revolved around the extent to which governments and the receiving or host populations encourage or discourage the preservation of minority cultures and / or religions. They increasingly pit those advocating some type of a multicultural model, one which values diversity and limits obstacles to its public expression, against France's republican model that fosters a dominant national identity, where the persistence of minority identities is seen as undercutting a common national culture. Often seen as the antithesis to multiculturalism, the republican model is usually associated with voluntary cultural assimilation by newcomers and their children.

At this point, you might be asking why all this is relevant to those engaged in counterterrorism. The importance attributed to resilient communities as an element in supporting the fight against terrorism is connected to the societal model of diversity. Does the idea of a resilient community run counter to models of diversity that view "communitarianism" (i.e., strong communal ties) as a threat to social cohesion? Evidence is insufficient to argue that either the "republican" or the multicultural model encourages radicalization. But it is true that there are important differences in attitudes towards communities on the basis of whether Canadians support either model. There are also important differences in attitudes between those favourable or unfavourable to the assimilation of religious minorities.

As shown in Charts 72 and 73, those who are more favourable to Canada's multicultural policy are more likely to hold positive views of Jews and Muslims. Those less favourable to the policy are also less likely to agree that if there is discrimination against Muslims and Jews, it is their own fault.

CHART 72 : CORRELATION : PERCENTAGE OF THOSE WHO TRUST MUSLIMS AND JEWS, AS SEEN BY THOSE WITH POSITIVE OR NEGATIVE VIEWS OF CANADIAN MULTICULTURAL POLICY

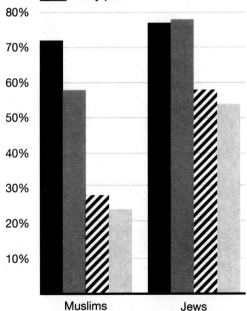

I have a very positive, somewhat positive, somewhat negative or very negative view of Canadian multicultural policy

- Very negative
- Somewhat negative
- Somewhat positive
- Very positive

AGREEMENT: THE FOLLOWING GROUP CAN BE TRUSTED

Source : ACS-Leger Marketing, March 2015

135

CHART 73 : CORRELATION : PERCENTAGE OF THOSE WHO AGREE THAT DISCRIMINATION AGAINST MUSLIMS AND JEWS IS MAINLY THEIR FAULT, AS SEEN BY THOSE WITH POSITIVE OR NEGATIVE VIEWS OF CANADIAN MULTICULTURAL POLICY

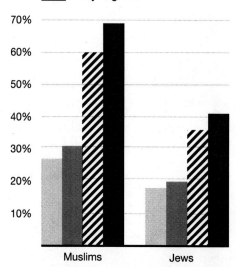

I have a very positive, somewhat positive, somewhat negative or very negative view of Canadian multicultural policy

Very positive
Somewhat positive
Somewhat negative
Very negative

AGREEMENT: DISCRMINATION AGAINST
THIS GROUP IS MAINLY THEIR FAULT

Source : ACS-Leger Marketing, March 2015

In theory, the idea of assimilation is very unpopular in Canada, as the Quebec and broader French-Canadian historic narratives frequently describe assimilation as the objective pursued by English Canada in its desire to diminish, if not altogether eliminate, the French language and culture from the public space. Canada's First Nations also regard assimilation as the long-standing objective of non-aboriginals. Hence many Canadian opinion leaders know the term has a negative connotation. But the important thing to be kept in mind in the republican concept is that assimilation is voluntary, however ambiguous that may appear. For the purposes of this analysis, we assume that republicans are more inclined to agree with the view that minorities should abandon their customs and traditions and become more like others, while advocates of multiculturalism would reject this view.

It might be assumed that the strongest opposition to assimilation would come from French Canada, and it is generally held that assimilation holds less appeal amongst Francophones outside of Quebec. Yet amongst Francophone Quebecers, one finds considerable support for the republican model. In Chart 74, a survey asking Canadians to select the model best suited, some one-third of Canadians support one of the key tenets of the republican model: the desire that minority religions abandon their customs and traditions. That view is held by a slight majority of Francophone Quebecers and shared by almost 30 percent of other Canadians.

CHART 74 : EXTENT TO WHICH CANADIANS AGREE THAT RELIGIOUS / CULTURAL GROUPS SUCH AS JEWS, MUSLIMS, AND SIKHS SHOULD ABANDON THEIR CUSTOMS AND TRADITIONS AND BECOME MORE LIKE OTHERS, BASED ON LANGUAGE

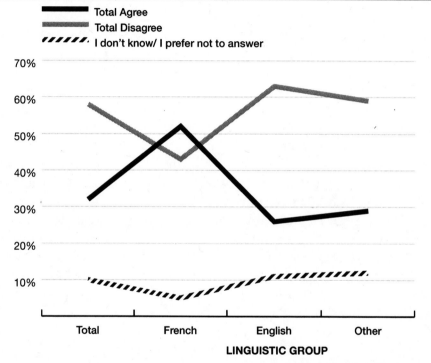

Source : ACS-Leger Marketing, March 2015

Chart 75 demonstrates that there is consistency in opinion across the age spectrum though, with the youngest cohort (18-24) much less attracted to the assimilation of religious minorities than the oldest cohort (65 and over).

CHART 75: EXTENT TO WHICH CANADIANS AGREE THAT RELIGIOUS / CULTURAL GROUPS SUCH AS JEWS, MUSLIMS, AND SIKHS SHOULD ABANDON THEIR CUSTOMS AND TRADITIONS AND BECOME MORE LIKE OTHERS, BASED ON AGE

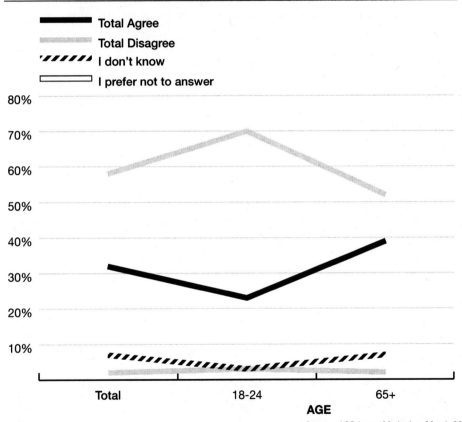

Source: ACS-Leger Marketing, March 2015

Table 8 considers how Canadians that reject or support assimilation view selected issues that are associated with the country's diversity. We assume that those persons supporting assimilation are more favourable to the republican model, while those unfavourable to assimilation are more sympathetic to multiculturalism. As observed, the assimilationists are far more persuaded that conflict between Muslims and the West is irreconcilable, that there are too many immigrants in Canada, and that public bans of religious symbols will reduce radicalization.

TABLE 8 : CORRELATION : PERCENTAGE OF THOSE WHO AGREE WITH SELECTED ISSUES ABOUT CANADA'S DIVERSITY, AS SEEN BY THOSE WHO AGREE OR DISAGREE THAT CERTAIN RELIGIOUS / CULTURAL GROUPS SHOULD ABANDON THEIR CUSTOMS AND TRADITIONS AND BECOME MORE LIKE OTHERS

Agreement: Religious/Cultural groups such as Jews, Muslims, and Sikhs should abandon their customs and traditions and become more like others				
	Strongly agree	Somewhat agree	Strongly agree	Somewhat agree
There is an irreconcilable conflict between Western societies and Islamic text and practices in the world	78%	75%	53%	36%
There are too many immigrants coming to Canada	69%	52%	33%	24%
Banning the wearing of visible religious symbols in public institutions will help reduce religious fundamentalism	70%	60%	30%	12%

Agreement: Religious/Cultural groups such as Jews, Muslims, and Sikhs should abandon their customs and traditions and become more like others				
	Strongly agree	Somewhat agree	Strongly agree	Somewhat agree
Banning the wearing of visible religious symbols in public institutions will encourage grievance and radicalization	39%	44%	47%	54%
I would be interested in participating in a dialogue between different religious groups	32%	38%	39%	44%

Source: ACS-Leger Marketing, March 2015

Another survey with a variation on the question of assimilation, referring to immigrants rather than religious minorities, points to similar differences in Canadian opinion on diversity, as seen in Chart 76. Those more favourable to immigrant assimilation hold more negative views of Muslims than those unfavourable to assimilation. On a lesser scale, support for assimilation also affects attitudes towards Jews.

CHART 76 : CORRELATION : PERCENTAGE OF THOSE WHO HAVE NEGATIVE OPINIONS OF JEWS AND MUSLIMS, AS SEEN BY THOSE WHO AGREE OR DISAGREE THAT IMMIGRANTS SHOULD BE ENCOURAGED TO GIVE UP THEIR CUSTOMS AND TRADITIONS AND BECOME MORE LIKE THE REST OF THE POPULATION

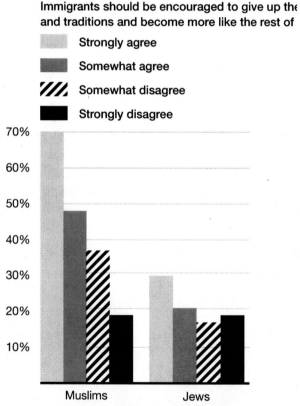

Immigrants should be encouraged to give up the
and traditions and become more like the rest of

Strongly agree

Somewhat agree

Somewhat disagree

Strongly disagree

**AGREEMENT: NEGATIVE OPINIONS OF
THE FOLLOWING GROUP**

Source : ACS-Leger Marketing, March 2013

In Table 9, we find that support or rejection of immigrant assimilation has no meaningful effect on the extent to which Canadians think terrorism can be justified. Also there is little difference in opinion about whether government counterterrorism efforts are working well. The big difference centres on the higher degree of concern expressed by assimilationists about the threat of terrorism in the country.

TABLE 9 : CORRELATION : PERCENTAGE OF THOSE WHO AGREE WITH SELECTED VIEWS AROUND TERRORISM, AS SEEN BY THOSE WHO AGREE OR DISAGREE THAT IMMIGRANTS SHOULD BE ENCOURAGED TO GIVE UP THEIR CUSTOMS AND TRADITIONS AND BECOME MORE LIKE THE REST OF THE POPULATION

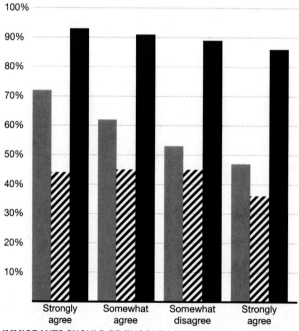

Worry about terrorist activities in Canada

■ Terrorism cannot be justified under any circumstances

/// Canadian government efforts to combat terrorism are working well

▨ Worried about terrorist activity in Canada

IMMIGRANTS SHOULD BE ENCOURAGED TO GIVE UP THEIR CUSTOMS AND TRADITIONS AND BECOME MORE LIKE THE REST OF THE POPULATION

Source : ACS-Leger Marketing, March 2012

CHAPTER 6

SECURITY, CIVIL LIBERTIES, AND RESPONSIBILITIES

When combating terrorism, must government suspend civil liberties to enable police, intelligence services, and military personnel to do what is necessary to protect citizens from domestic and foreign threats and to minimize violence and threats to infrastructure? Must governments risk the temptation of compromising civil liberties? Should the protection of civil liberties not be a priority if it is so central a tenet of our liberal democracy?

The response to this debate is critical to the real and perceived impact of counterterrorism on our cultural identities, and its outcome will have an effect on our broader vision of what it means to live in a multicultural democracy.

It is common practice for civil liberties to be restricted (or that restrictions be proposed) during times of high anxiety in democratic societies. Ghosh and Bhui (2012) point out that concern about terrorism has changed in relation to the immediacy of an attack. Huddy, Khatib, and Capelos (2002) found that, after 9/11, there was a sharp increase in the level of concern with regard to terrorism, but by early 2002 (Huddy, Feldman, Capelos, and Provost, 2002), concerns about being a victim of terrorism fell back to levels expressed prior to 9/11.

In Australia, following the Bali bombings in 2002 and 2005, which were the most significant terrorist attack involving Australian citizens, concern peaked after both attacks but subsided thereafter (Cummins, Mellor, Stokes, and Lau, 2005). These observations are consistent with analysis previously provided.

The same holds true for public calls for more action in the fight against terrorism, as they too may fluctuate in the aftermath of high profile incidents of terrorism resulting in the consideration of measures that may compromise civil liberties.

A crisis in which people fear that their security is threatened may force a reassessment of civil liberties, where the trade-off to gain a sense of greater personal safety is evident (Nacos, Bloch-Elkon, and Shapiro, 2011).

This issue is complicated by growing uncertainty about what constitutes a violation of civil liberties not only on the part of important segments of the population, but also among the jurists tasked with their interpretation. Our focus is not on the interpretation itself, but on how, in the midst of the debates around counterterrorism, there is growing ambiguity in public opinion about the restriction of civil liberties.

There appears to be no clear end in sight to the fight against terrorism. It may be difficult to reverse actions to fight terrorism. Hence a temporary suspension of civil liberties in support of counterterrorism risks becoming something more permanent, restricting civil liberties as a response to high public anxiety.

RESTRICTING CIVIL LIBERTIES

There is relatively serious concern amongst Canadians about the loss of civil liberties. Some two-third of Canadians report being very or somewhat worried about the prospect of restricting civil liberties for counterterrorism purposes. Persons identifying with no religion and persons identifying themselves as Christians, Jews, and Muslims share roughly the same level of concern, thus making a consensus on the issue. Analysts have observed that the presence of a terrorist threat generally increases support for restrictions on civil liberties (Davis and Silver, 2004). Our surveys confirm this relationship, as seen in Chart 77, given that those Canadians more willing to sacrifice civil liberties are more worried about terrorist activities in Canada than those less inclined to give up civil liberties.

CHART 77 : CORRELATION : PERCENTAGE OF THOSE WHO WORRIED ABOUT TERRORIST ACTIVITIES IN CANADA, AS SEEN BY THOSE WHO AGREE OR DISAGREE THAT THEY ARE READY TO GIVE UP SOME CIVIL LIBERTIES TO CURB TERRORISM

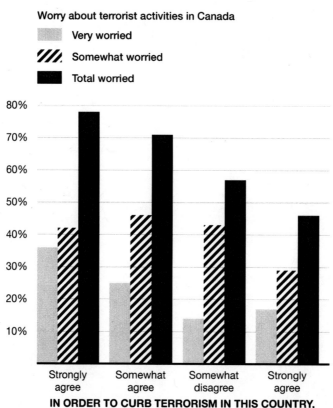

Worry about terrorist activities in Canada

Very worried

Somewhat worried

Total worried

IN ORDER TO CURB TERRORISM IN THIS COUNTRY,
I AM READY TO GIVE UP SOME CIVIL LIBERTIES

Source : ACS-Leger Marketing, January 2014

Our surveys over the period 2012–2015 reveal that, on average, one in three Canadians agree that they are willing to give up some civil liberties to combat terrorism. A rise in such willingness appeared in the period of January 2015 in the aftermath of the terrorist attacks on the offices of Charlie Hebdo and Hyper Cacher in Paris, as 40 percent of Canadians agreed that they were ready to give up some civil liberties to curb terrorism. But by the third week of March 2015, the national figure returned closer to the benchmark at 35 percent. In general, as seen in Chart 78, younger Canadians are less likely than older ones to be willing to sacrifice civil liberties and women less so than men. Indeed, a majority of Canadians over the age of 65 consistently agree with giving up civil liberties to curb terrorism.

CHART 78 : EXTENT TO WHICH CANADIANS AGREE THAT IN ORDER TO CURB TERRORISM IN CANADA, THEY ARE READY TO GIVE UP SOME CIVIL LIBERTIES

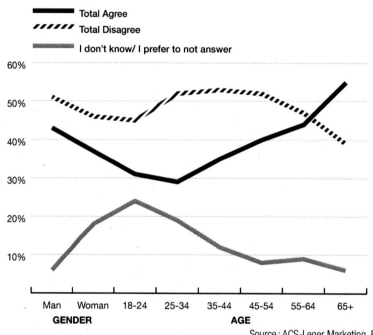

Source : ACS-Leger Marketing, February 2015

As mentioned previously, the difference in the willingness of older Canadians to sacrifice civil liberties in support of counterterrorism is likely attributable to their higher perception of the threat of terrorism. Surveys have also revealed that the perception of the threat of terrorism was closely connected to whether Canadians felt that there was an irreconcilable conflict between Western and Muslim societies, as seen in Chart 79. Stronger adherents to the irreconcilable conflict thesis are far more ready to cede civil liberties.

CHART 79 : CORRELATION : PERCENTAGE OF THOSE WHO AGREE
THAT THEY ARE READY TO GIVE UP SOME CIVIL LIBERTIES TO CURB
TERRORISM, AS SEEN BY THOSE WHO AGREE OR DISAGREE THAT
THERE IS AN IRRECONCILABLE CONFLICT BETWEEN WESTERN
SOCIETIES AND THE MUSLIM RELIGION IN THE WORLD

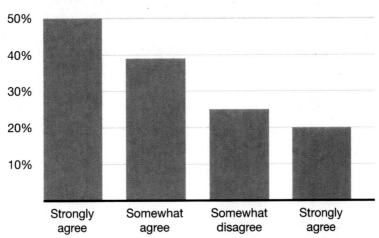

**THERE IS AN IRRECONCILABLE CONFLICT BETWEEN WESTERN
SOCIETIES AND THE MUSLIM RELIGION IN THE WORLD**

Source : ACS-Leger Marketing, February 2015

Chart 80 shows that those willing to sacrifice civil liberties are far more likely to believe that the Government of Canada and international authorities are effective in the ongoing fight against terrorism, while those least prepared to sacrifice civil liberties are least confident in efforts to combat terrorism. One might think that the inverse would hold true and that recourse to weaken civil liberties would be a sign that counterterrorism is not working well. But instead, the sacrifice of civil liberties on the part of the government seems to reassure important segments of the population that the matter is being taken with the utmost seriousness.

CHART 80 : CORRELATION : PERCENTAGE OF THOSE WHO AGREE THAT COUNTERTERRORISM MEASURES NATIONALLY AND INTERNATIONALLY ARE WORKING WELL, AS SEEN BY THOSE WHO AGREE OR DISAGREE THAT IN ORDER TO CURB TERRORISM, THEY ARE READY TO GIVE UP SOME CIVIL LIBERTIES

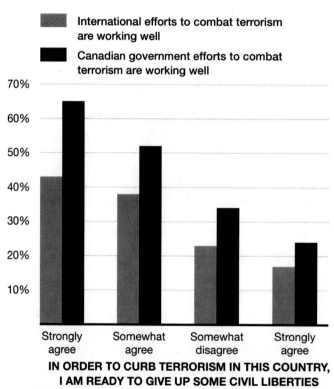

International efforts to combat terrorism are working well

Canadian government efforts to combat terrorism are working well

IN ORDER TO CURB TERRORISM IN THIS COUNTRY, I AM READY TO GIVE UP SOME CIVIL LIBERTIES

Source : ACS-Leger Marketing, February 2015

But one area where the gap is not as substantial is in the relationship between opinion about Muslims and the willingness to sacrifice civil liberties.

JACK JEDWAB

COUNTERTERRORISM: CIVIL RIGHTS VERSUS INTRUSION

There often appears confusion amongst Canadians on what constitutes a violation of civil liberties and what is highly intrusive. In examining public opinion, the line between the two sometimes seems blurred. Yet identifying that line should be important to those that are tasked with responsibility for counterterrorism. In an essay on *Balancing Security and Liberty within the European Human Rights Framework*, De Hert raises a number of helpful questions in this regard. He asks "what standards make one practice less intrusive than another? How can we measure intrusiveness? Is something or some power more intrusive when it touches upon a wide range of rights and liberties? Or, when it deeply impacts upon one right or liberty? When it is applied without judicial intervention? When there is no immediate harm but potential harm in the future?" (De Hert, 2015, p. 94).

Answers to these questions are far more complex than what is offered here. Rather, one might gauge some insight on the basis of what Canadians regard as intrusive and what there is agreement upon across the spectrum of religious identification. In four areas that have been measured, in Table 10, there is a fair bit of consensus. A majority of Canadians are favourable to expanding camera surveillance on streets and in public places. Canadians are divided around the idea of requiring that everyone carry a national identity card to show a police officer upon request. Catholics (54 percent) and Muslims (52 percent) are more supporting of the idea than Jews (41 percent) and persons not identifying with a religion (38 percent).

But the majority of Canadians are clearly unfavourable to a series of proposals that are likely viewed as too intrusive and probably seen as infringing on civil liberties. They include such measures as collecting data on domestic phone calls and looking at individuals' calling patterns, regularly monitoring the telephone calls and emails of citizens, and the imprisonment of people suspected of terrorism without a trial — a proposition that Canada's Muslim population rejects even more vehemently.

TABLE 10 : EXTENT TO WHICH CANADIANS AGREE WITH
EXPANDING SELECTED COUNTERTERRORISM MEASURES

In dealing with issues of security and the prevention of terrorism, the government should...	Total Agree
Expand camera surveillance on streets and in public places	67%
Require everyone to carry a national identity card at all times to show a police officer upon request	47%
Collect data on domestic phone calls and look at individuals calling patterns	30%
Regularly monitor the telephone calls and emails of citizens	21%
Possess the right to put people suspected of terrorism in prison without a trial	23%

Source : ACS-Leger Marketing, March 2013

On the question of mandatory identity cards in Chart 81, a majority of those Canadians that somewhat agree with sacrificing civil liberties do not support this idea.

CHART 81 : CORRELATION : PERCENTAGE OF THOSE WHO AGREE THAT THE GOVERNMENT SHOULD REQUIRE EVERYONE TO CARRY A NATIONAL IDENTITY CARD AT ALL TIMES TO SHOW IT TO THE POLICE UPON REQUEST, AS SEEN BY THOSE WHO AGREE OR DISAGREE THAT THEY ARE READY TO GIVE UP SOME CIVIL LIBERTIES TO CURB TERRORISM

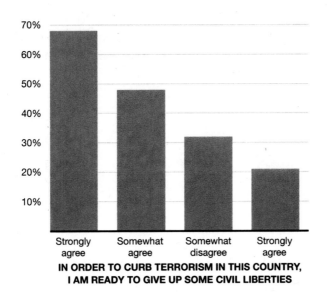

IN ORDER TO CURB TERRORISM IN THIS COUNTRY, I AM READY TO GIVE UP SOME CIVIL LIBERTIES

Source : ACS-Leger Marketing, March 2013

It is worth noting that the largest plurality of Canadians (45 percent) surveyed believe that the government is at present regularly monitoring the phone calls, emails and financial transactions of citizens. Some 25 percent of Canadians do not believe this to be the case, and 30 percent do not offer their opinion.

There are two areas where Muslims disapprove to a much greater degree

COUNTERTERRORISM AND IDENTITIES : CANADIAN VIEWPOINTS

than do other Canadians, as seen in Chart 82. A majority of the population support the idea of making it more difficult for people to come across our national borders. The proposal yields the support of 40 percent of the Muslims surveyed. Those identifying with no religion are divided on the issue, with the rate of approval noticeably below the national average. On a related issue, a majority of Canadians disapprove of requiring certain religious minorities to undergo more intensive security checks. While the idea garners approval from 40 percent of Canadians, it is supported by less than one in four Canadian Muslims. The simple explanation for the more intense opposition to these proposals on the part of Muslims is that they likely feel that they are a particular target of such measures.

CHART 82 : CANADIANS AGREE WITH SELECT GOVERNMENT COUNTERTERRORISM MEASURES IN DEALING WITH ISSUES OF SECURITY AND THE PREVENTION OF TERRORISM

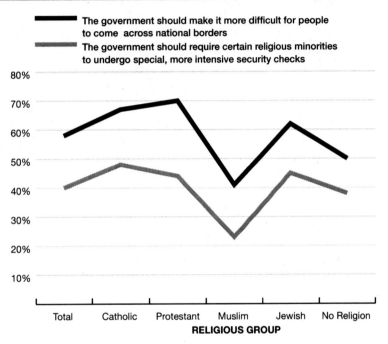

——— The government should make it more difficult for people to come across national borders

——— The government should require certain religious minorities to undergo special, more intensive security checks

RELIGIOUS GROUP

Source : ACS-Leger Marketing, March 2013

CIVIL LIBERTIES AND LIMITS
ON THE RIGHTS OF CITIZENS

Although the majority of Canadians are not in favour of sacrificing their civil liberties in support of counterterrorism, they do not condone protecting the civil liberties of those who are suspected of involvement with terrorism, as seen in Chart 83. This can be a rather slippery slope, as Canada has traditionally operated on the basis of the presumption of innocence and a call for due process. That said, such issues are increasingly tied in the minds of the public to concerns over foreign fighters and to international attention obtained by the Islamic State (ISIS-ISIL).

CHART 83 : EXTENT TO WHICH CANADIANS AGREE THAT IF
SOMEONE IS SUSPECTED OF INVOLVEMENT WITH TERRORISM,
THEY SHOULD NOT BE PROTECTED BY HUMAN RIGHTS LAW

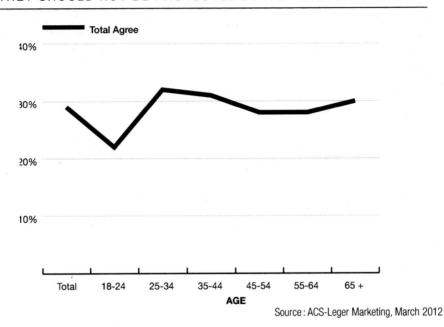

Source : ACS-Leger Marketing, March 2012

The domestic concern with these foreign fighters is not limited to sympa-
thizers of ISIS-ISIL going overseas to fight, but also with them participating in
acts of terrorism if and/or when they return to Canada. Our surveys reveal, in
Chart 84, that the majority of Canadians believe that the government has no
responsibility to protect, help re-integrate, or provide other services to Canadian
citizens who choose to fight with a foreign army (e.g., Syria or Iraq). However,
a gap emerged on the basis of age, with those under 35 being divided over
the issue and those above the age far more inclined to agree with severing

ties with such individuals. Again this is likely a function of differences in the perception of the threat from terrorism.

CHART 84 : EXTENT TO WHICH CANADIANS AGREE THAT THE GOVERNMENT OF CANADA HAS NO RESPONSIBILITY FOR CITIZENS OF OUR COUNTRY THAT CHOOSE TO FIGHT WITH A FOREIGN ARMY

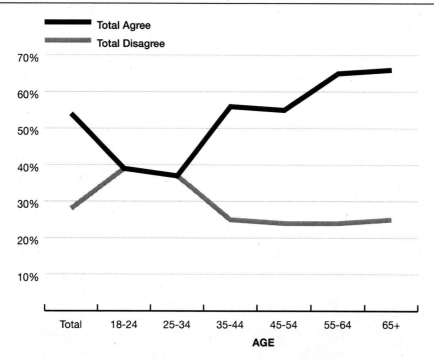

Source : ACS-Leger Marketing, September 2014

In response to what are referred to as foreign fighters, and to send a message to those who might consider fighting alongside a terrorist group abroad, efforts have been undertaken by certain governments to revoke the citizenship of such individuals. In 2014, the United Kingdom introduced legislation that allowed citizenship to be stripped, even if this made the individuals stateless. The Government of Canada has moved to invalidate the passports of those who have chosen to fight with designated terrorist movements abroad.

Nearly 50 percent of Canadians agree that foreign fighters should indeed lose their citizenship, as seen in Chart 85. It is worth noting that one in five Canadians do not express an opinion on the matter, which is likely a function of the difficulty in comprehending it. Younger Canadians are less likely to endorse removing the citizenship of such individuals, but are somewhat less likely to express an opinion on the issue. Muslim Canadians, who likely feel that they may be the target of such measures, are more divided over the issue.

CHART 85 : EXTENT TO WHICH CANADIANS AGREE THAT REGARDLESS OF THE MERITS OF THE CAUSE, CANADIANS THAT FIGHT WITH A NON-STATE ARMED GROUP SHOULD LOSE THEIR CITIZENSHIP

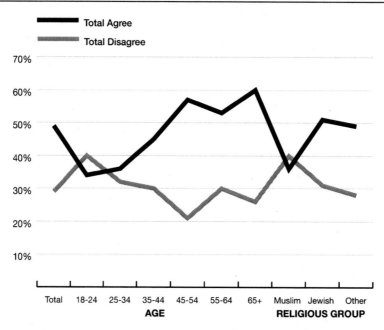

Source : ACS-Leger Marketing, January 2014

As revealed in Chart 86, even those Canadians who are the least inclined to sacrifice civil liberties are mostly supportive of the stripping of citizenship from foreign fighters.

CHART 86 : CORRELATION : PERCENTAGE OF THOSE WHO AGREE THAT THE GOVERNMENT OF CANADA SHOULD REMOVE CITIZENSHIP FROM CANADIANS THAT GO ABROAD TO FIGHT WITH A FOREIGN ARMY, AS SEEN BY THOSE WHO AGREE OR DISAGREE THAT THEY ARE READY TO GIVE UP SOME CIVIL LIBERTIES TO CURB TERRORISM

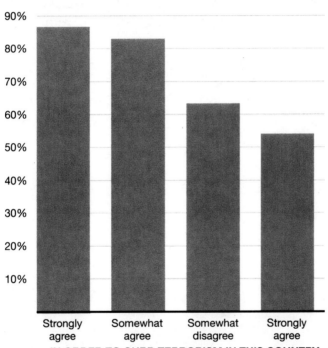

IN ORDER TO CURB TERRORISM IN THIS COUNTRY, I AM READY TO GIVE UP SOME CIVIL LIBERTIES

Source : ACS-Leger Marketing, January 2014

FREEDOM OF RELIGION AND COUNTERTERRORISM

As seen in Chart 87, most Canadians are not worried about the loss of their right to practise their faith. Overall, some 30 percent have expressed concerns in that regard, but a majority of Muslims feel otherwise, with some 52 percent indicating such concern.

CHART 87 : EXTENT TO WHICH CANADIANS ARE WORRIED ABOUT THE LOSS OF THEIR RIGHT TO PRACTISE THEIR FAITH

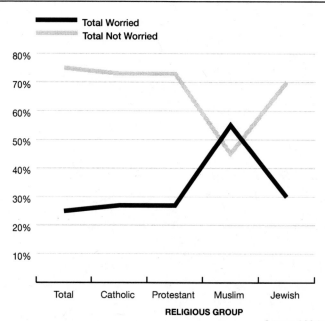

Source : ACS-Leger Marketing, March 2013

To some Muslims, the concerns may appear warranted when considering the percentage of Canadians prepared to limit freedom of religion in the fight against terrorism, as indicated in Chart 88. While one in three Canadians are prepared to give up some civil liberties to support counterterrorism, approximately 45 percent of the population agree that limits to freedom of religion are necessary in the fight against terrorism, and 40 percent agree that limits to freedom of expression are necessary in the fight against terrorism. Not surprisingly, those most willing to give up civil liberties are most likely to agree with limits to freedom of religion and expression. Amongst those that are somewhat reticent to give up civil liberties, some 40 percent favour limits to freedom of religion in the fight against terrorism.

CHART 88 : CORRELATION : PERCENTAGE OF THOSE WHO AGREE IN LIMITING FREEDOMS TO FIGHT TERRORISM, AS SEEN BY THOSE WHO AGREE OR DISAGREE THAT THEY ARE READY TO GIVE UP SOME CIVIL LIBERTIES TO CURB TERRORISM

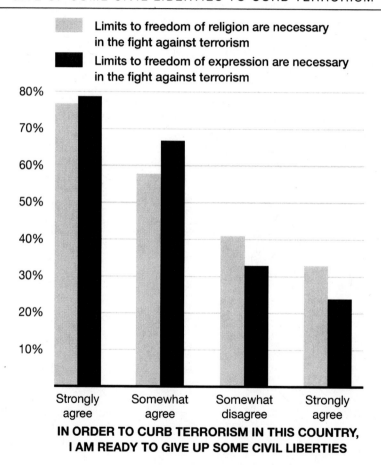

IN ORDER TO CURB TERRORISM IN THIS COUNTRY, I AM READY TO GIVE UP SOME CIVIL LIBERTIES

Source : ACS-Leger Marketing, March 2015

The debate in Quebec around the Charter of Values promoted the idea that the public expression of religion — notably by members of the province's minorities — risked encouraging "radicalized" behaviour. Hence, curbing the visible display of religious symbols would serve to diminish the potential for such behaviour. Architects of the Quebec Charter, like former Parti Québécois Minister Bernard Drainville, implied that such a ban was a form of counterterrorism (Croteau and Lessard, 2015). It was further implied that those wearing religious symbols were marginalizing themselves and as such were becoming more vulnerable to the process of radicalization.

Outside of Quebec, when surveyed in March 2015, some 45 percent of respondents believed that such bans were more likely to encourage grievance and radicalization, compared to 35 percent who felt otherwise. Francophone Quebecers were more likely to take an opposing view, with 50 percent believing that such measures would not encourage grievance and radicalization, while 40 percent felt otherwise. Quebecers were somewhat more likely to agree (47 percent) than to disagree (43 percent) that banning the wearing of visible religious symbols in public institutions will help reduce religious fundamentalism. That view was not shared by other Canadians, with 50 percent disagreeing that such a ban would reduce radicalization and 30 percent holding the opposing view (some 20 percent offered no response).

Across the spectrum more Canadians agree than disagree that measures such as bans of religious symbols would encourage grievances and radicalization than have the contrary effect (Chart 89).

CHAT 89 : CORRELATION : PERCENTAGE OF THOSE WHO AGREE
AND DISAGREE WITH THE NOTION THAT BANNING THE WEARING
OF VISIBLE RELIGIOUS SYMBOLS IN PUBLIC INSTITUTIONS
WILL ENCOURAGE GRIEVANCE AND RADICALIZATION, AS SEEN
BY THOSE WHO AGREE OR DISAGREE THAT THEY ARE READY
TO GIVE UP SOME CIVIL LIBERTIES TO CURB TERRORISM

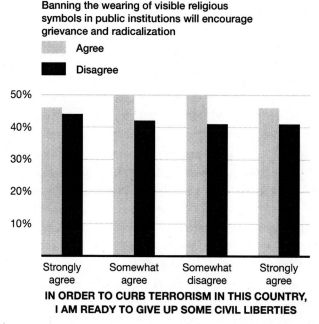

Banning the wearing of visible religious
symbols in public institutions will encourage
grievance and radicalization

Agree

Disagree

IN ORDER TO CURB TERRORISM IN THIS COUNTRY,
I AM READY TO GIVE UP SOME CIVIL LIBERTIES

Source : ACS-Leger Marketing, March 2015

When Canada's Jews and Muslims were asked, the overwhelming majority
disagreed that such a ban would reduce radicalization, as depicted in Chart 90.

CHART 90 : EXTENT TO WHICH CANADIANS AGREE THAT BANNING THE WEARING OF VISIBLE SYMBOLS IN PUBLIC INSTITUTIONS WILL HELP REDUCE RELIGIOUS FUNDAMENTALISM

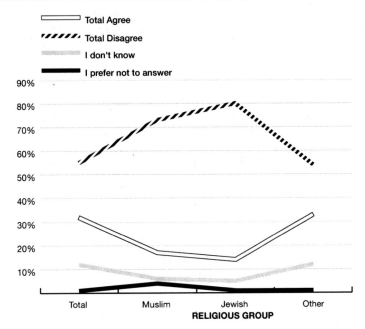

Source : ACS-Leger Marketing, March 2015

Discussions of counterterrorism in conjunction with identities cannot avoid directing considerable attention at the status of civil liberties in Canada. Interpretations and decisions about civil liberties have defined the status of individuals within our society and the communities with which they identify. It is fundamentally important to strike a balance between the government's commitment to ensuring the public's safety and its commitment to safeguarding the civil rights of the public.

When these objectives are cast as undermining each other, many Canadians should feel uneasy, and ultimately some will feel this more so than others. It's apparent that in the immediate aftermath of a terrorist incident, governments feel compelled to act quickly to quell public anxiety, and such action may arise at the expense of civil liberties. Effectiveness in counterterrorism will not operate by surveys of public opinion, but at the same time to ignore such opinion risks undermining confidence in those charged with our collective security.

There is no doubt that we're in for the long term in the fight against terrorism, leaving us with more than ample time for deliberation and greater public engagement in discussion about our commitment to civil liberties and the trade-offs that might be made in this regard. That conversation must be ongoing and inclusive if we are to entrust our officials with so vital a mandate.

CONCLUSION

Comprehending evolving levels of anxiety amongst Canadians over the threat of terrorism was the point of departure for this book. It is no surprise that in the aftermath of the September 11 terrorist attacks, there was a sharp increase in anxieties in the United States and elsewhere. Nearly fifteen years later, the level of anxiety has fluctuated, and in Canada today that level is only somewhat lower than it was back in 2001.

Our research reveals that the spectre of 9/11 still haunts much of the population in the nation to the north of the World Trade Centre. Anxiety is subject to fluctuations and usually peaks shortly after a terrorist attack. In the case of Canadians, from the beginning of 2013 to the end of 2014, anxiety over terrorism rose from 44 to 63 percent (with 20 percent saying they were very worried and 43 percent somewhat worried). The threat of terrorism will inevitably give rise to anxiety, and it's hard to establish its normal level.

Since it's unrealistic to assume an outright elimination of terrorism, continued anxieties are to be expected. The best to be hoped for is to diminish the incidence of terrorism and/or persuade the public that the threat is under control. The latter will likely require a change in the public's perception of the threat.

Significant changes to the level of anxiety are not without consequences in terms of how society chooses to address the threat and the kind of resources it deploys to that end. When suffering from anxiety, it's important to identify its symptoms. When asked to define terrorism, Canadians came up with a multitude of responses. With regard to actions being taken to fight terrorism, our surveys reveal that many Canadians are unaware of what is being done.

Much of the discussion about terrorism and counterterrorism is framed as a question of identity. For confirmation of this, one need simply follow the evolving language often used to describe the issues. After 9/11 there was talk about the conflict of civilizations, debate about the root causes of terrorism, and calls by opinion leaders for greater social cohesion.

More recently, imported conflicts, home-grown terrorists, foreign fighters, de-radicalization, and countering violent extremism have dominated conversations about the intersection between security and identity. When identity is discussed in relation to such security concerns, it's religion that almost always comes to the top of mind, and the conversation nearly always turns to the Islamic faith.

The identity dimension of the national security-identity paradigm takes multiple forms. There are different ways of framing the issue of identity, and clearly some are more constructive than others. Some framing is downright unhelpful, notably when it encourages oversimplification and/or generalizations about communities.

In discussions of religion, too often the connection made between identity and security does not consider the internal diversity or pluralism of the group, preferring instead to lump everyone in together. Identification with a religious group does not tell us anything about a person's level of adherence and practice. Nor do we learn much about the importance they attribute to other dimensions of their identities.

Contrary to what some observers assume, our data has found that the more someone is attached to their religious group, the more they are attached to Canada. This may seem counterintuitive to those who insist that ethnic and religious identities are inevitably in conflict with Canadian identity and that a good dose of "our" values — the ones we share — will help rectify the problem.

While some see religious identities and their expression as the source of the threat of terrorism, others see it as part of the solution. The data makes it quite clear that it's predominantly the fundamentalist expression of Islam that is contributing to the rising anxieties about terrorism in Canada.

A collateral effect of this perception is that persons reporting much higher than average levels of anxiety are far more inclined to see religion as divisive and less likely to see religious pluralism as an asset for the society. They are most likely to feel the lingering effects of 9/11 (they may fear it could happen again), they are persuaded that there is an irreconcilable conflict between the West and Muslims, they are very worried about the relationship between Muslims and non-Muslims, and they generally hold more negative views of Muslims. They report lower levels of trust in Muslims (though they are less likely to have met a Muslim).

They also want more social cohesion, by which they mean greater assimilation of minority religious groups (they're more apt to agree with the view that "they" need to become more like "us"), and would endorse policies curbing the public expression of religion.

While we somewhat caution against caricature, the most anxious Canadians are more open to accepting limits to freedom of religion, and many see this as a counterterrorism measure. In general, they are far more willing than the less anxious to cede civil liberties to fight terrorism and — as an example — more supportive of special security checks at borders for religious minorities (in other words, Muslims). They are most likely to support a military solution as the only way to deal with the problem of terrorism.

That said, they express concern about the level of anti-Muslim sentiment and are relatively supportive of certain soft counterterrorism measures such as dialogue between leaders of religious communities. This most anxious group is generally an older demographic that is far more likely to offer an opinion on issues. A small minority of Canadian Muslims frame the issues similarly and also express high levels of anxiety.

In response to the security-identity paradigm, those who see religion as part of the solution believe that when individuals feel comfortable about "who they are," they feel less pressure to abandon their identities and hence they will be less at risk of radicalization.

Those less anxious are somewhat more inclined to attach value to religion and/or they do not see its expression as a serious social problem. They are more inclined to see religious pluralism as an asset and are less likely to associate religion with fundamentalism.

The less anxious are generally a younger demographic, and they are less affected by the spectre of 9/11 (they think less about whether it could happen again). They are less convinced that there is an irreconcilable conflict between the West and Muslims, but a significant minority do subscribe to this idea. They are not as worried as those most anxious about the relationship between Muslims and non-Muslims, but they do acknowledge the important challenge arising from the relationship.

They are less favourable to giving up civil liberties to combat terrorism (and hence less likely to support greater security checks for religious minorities). They are much less likely to harbour negative views of Muslims and more inclined to report that they either often or sometimes have contact with them. They are very concerned about anti-Muslim sentiment. They are much less favourable to assimilation of minority religious groups and reject policies curbing the public expression of religion. They worry about threats to freedom of religion.

There is a large share of Canadians that fall somewhere in the middle of the overall profiles offered above of the most and least anxious. Those in the middle reflect some degree of ambivalence on the part of much of the Canadian population when it comes to responses to terrorism. This is reflected in the views of the many Canadians who believe in dialogue, which includes many who think that there is an irreconcilable conflict between Muslims and the West;

this line of "reasoning" has been described as reconcilable irreconcilability.

On the spectrum from the most to least anxious, most Canadian Muslims are more likely to fall into the less anxious category. In itself, that perception may be looked upon with suspicion by the most anxious. Still there are shared perspectives across the spectrum from the most to the least anxious. There is a strong sense of attachment to Canada (except amongst Francophone Quebecers for issues secondary to the topic of this publication).

There is widespread agreement that under no circumstances can terrorism be justified, regardless of its perceived causes. There is a high level of trust in the police, the armed forces and the justice system (in contrast to what we may hear by way of anecdotes). Despite these areas of convergence, it will be difficult to bridge the gap between the most and least anxious.

Our surveys point to a relatively high level of communal responsibility when it comes to condemning reprehensible acts committed by one or more individuals from a community with which someone identifies. But such commitment notwithstanding, it is wrong to hold all community members accountable for the actions of a small minority of individuals. That may be the responsibility of certain leaders, notably if individuals say their actions were taken in the name of the group, but identifying as a Catholic, Protestant, Jew, or Muslim should not require you to denounce acts by those identifying with the same group. To demand otherwise risks fuelling mistrust of members of specific communities. It prompts stigmatization by legitimizing a test of an individual's views on issues where it is within their right not to be tested — the right to be disengaged.

There is a growing interest in the development and delivery of narratives or story lines to counter the dissemination of extremist ideologies that encourage criminal activity. These counter-narratives are seen as a form of counterterrorism, as they aim to prevent domestic perpetrators. It can't be assumed that narratives that succeed within a vacuum are so internal to a community that the broader societal context — its narrative — has no bearing on the identity formation of at-risk individuals. In this regard, a counter-narrative enjoys higher credibility when it is compatible with a broader societal narrative guarding against stigmatization. This is helpful in building trust in institutions and individuals responsible for public safety.

Vague and ambiguous talk about shared values has not proven to be successful in enhancing attachment or diminishing anxieties. Indeed, too often such discourse disguises the "us and them" paradigm and is more likely to be counterproductive. The debate around Quebec's Charter of Values serves as a prime example of just how divisive talk about shared values can be and the damage it can do to relations between communities.

LIST OF CHARTS AND TABLES

BIBLIOGRAPHY

Bauböck, R. (March 01, 2002). "Farewell to Multiculturalism? Sharing Values and Identities in Societies of Immigration." *Journal of International Migration and Integration / Revue de l'intégration et de la migration internationale*, 3, 1, 1–16.

Bergin, A., and Murphy, C. (April 15, 2015). "Time to Sound the Alarm on Terror Alerts." *The Australian*. Retrieved from http://www.theaustralian.com.au/opinion/time-to-sound-the-alarm-on-terror-alerts/story-e6frg6zo-1227303902333.

Bjørgo, T. (2005). *Root Causes of Terrorism: Myths, Reality, and Ways Forward*. London: Routledge.

Briggs, R., Fieschi, C., and Lownsbrough, H. (2006). "Bringing It Home: Community-based Approaches to Counter-terrorism." *Demos*. London: Magdalen House.

Brooks D. (March 03, 2011). "Huntington's Clash Revisited." The New York Times. Retrieved from http://www.nytimes.com/2011/03/04/opinion/04brooks.html?_r=0.

Canadian Security and Intelligence Services. (June 09, 2015). Featured. *Canadian Security and Intelligence Services*. Retrieved from https://www.csis.gc.ca/index-en.php.

Carment, D., and Prest, S. (April 23, 2013). "Finding 'Root Causes' of Terrorism Is the Core of Canadian Policy." *The Globe and Mail*. Retrieved from http://www.theglobeandmail.com/globe-debate/finding-root-causes-of-terrorism-is-the-core-of-canadian-policy/article11494674/.

CBC News. (March 10, 2015). "Denis Coderre Defends Anti-radicalization Plans." CBC *News*. Retrieved from http://www.cbc.ca/news/canada/montreal/denis-coderre-defends-anti-radicalization-plans-1.2988752.

Chebel, A. A., and Reich, S. (2010). *Managing Ethnic Diversity after 9/11: Integration, Security, and Civil Liberties in Transatlantic Perspective.* New Brunswick: Rutgers University Press.

Croteau, M., and Lessard, D. (January 13, 2015). "Charte de la laïcité: « une clause grand-père » prévaudra." *La Presse*. Retrieved from http://www.lapresse.ca/actualites/politique/politique-quebecoise/201501/12/01-4834573-charte-de-la-laicite-une-clause-grand-pere-prevaudra.php.

Cummins, R. A., Mellor, D., Stokes, M. A., and Lau, A. (2008). "Quality of Life Down-Under: The Australian Unity Wellbeing Index." In A. C. Michalos, D. Huschka, and V. Møller (Eds.), *Barometers of Quality of Life Around the Globe: How Are We Doing?* (pp. 135–159). Dordrecht: Springer.

Davis. D. W., and Silver, B. D. (January 2004). "Civil Liberties vs. Security: Public Opinion in the Context of the Terrorist Attacks on America." *American Journal of Political Science*, 48, 1, 28–46.

Dawson, L. L., and Bramadat, P. (Eds.). (2014). *Religious Radicalization and Securitization in Canada and Beyond.* Toronto: University of Toronto Press.

Dearden, L. (July 20, 2015). "David Cameron Extremism Speech: Read the Transcript in Full." The Independent. Retrieved from http://www.independent.co.uk/news/uk/politics/david-cameron-extremism-speech-read-the-transcript-in-full-10401948.html.

De Hert, P. (September 2015). "Balancing Security and Liberty within the European Human Rights Framework: A Critical Reading of the Court's Case Law in the Light of Surveillance and Criminal Law Enforcement Strategies after 9/11." *Utrecht Law Review,* 1, 1, 68–96.

Douglas, E., and Wentz, N. (n.d.). "Terrorism in the Middle East: A Clash of Cultures." *Unpublished Paper.* Retrieved from http://web.stanford.edu/class/e297a/Terrorism%20in%20the%20Middle%20East%20-%20A%20Clash%20of%20Cultures.doc.

El-Said, H. (February 24, 2015). "In Defence of Soft Power: Why a 'War' on Terror Will Never Win." *New Statesman.* Retrieved from http://www.newstatesman.com/politics/2015/02/defence-soft-power-why-war-terror-will-never-win.

Environics Research Group. (December 2006). *Focus Canada: Report 2006–4.* Retrieved from http://www.environicsinstitute.org/uploads/institute-projects/focus%20canada%202006-4%20report.pdf.

Federal Emergency Management Agency. (February 2015). "Improving the Public's Awareness and Reporting of Suspicious Activity: Key Research

Findings from Literature Review, Household Surveys, Focus Groups and Interviews." U.S. *Department of Homeland Security, Federal Emergency Management Agency, National Preparedness Directorate.*

Fletcher, G.P. (2006). "The Indefinable Concept of Terrorism." *Journal of International Criminal Justice, 4,* 894.

Flynn-Piercy, H. (August 30, 2011). "Huntington's Clash of Civilizations." *E-International Relations Students*. Retrieved from http://www.e-ir.info/2011/08/30/huntingtons-clash-of-civilizations/.

Ghosh, P., and Bhui, K. (Fall 2012). "Perspectives on Security, Terrorism and Counter-terrorism." Canadian Diversity, 9, 4, 11–13.

Government of Canada. (2013). *Building Resilience against Terrorism: Canada's Counterterrorism Strategy* (2nd ed.). Retrieved from http://www.publicsafety.gc.ca/cnt/rsrcs/pblctns/rslnc-gnst-trrrsm/rslnc-gnst-trrrsm-eng.pdf.

Heath, J. (2003). *The Myth of Shared Values in Canada*. Ottawa: Canadian Centre for Management Development.

Hoffman, B. (1998). *Inside Terrorism*. New York: Columbia University Press.

Homeland Security. (2015). "If You See Something, Say Something." Homeland Security. Retrieved from http://www.dhs.gov/see-something-say-something.

Huddy, L., Feldman, S., Capelos, T., and Provost, C. (September 01, 2002). "The Consequences of Terrorism: Disentangling the Effects of Personal and National Threat." *Political Psychology*, 23, 3, 485–509.

Huddy, L., Khatib, N., and Capelos, T. (2002). "The Polls — Trends Reactions to the Terrorist Attacks of September 11, 2001." *Public Opinion Quarterly*, 66, 418–450.

Huntington, S. P. (1996). The Clash of Civilizations and the *Remaking of World Order.* New York: Simon and Schuster.

Jacofsky, M. D., Santos, M.T., Khemlani-Patel, S., and Neziroglu, F. (August 09, 2013). "Normal and Abnormal Anxiety: What's the Difference?" *American Addiction Centers*. Retrieved from https://www.mentalhelp.net/articles/normal-and-abnormal-anxiety-what-s-the-difference/.

Jedwab , J. (July 02, 2010). "Canadians' Preferred Rhetoric: What Words and Phrases Resonate Most with Canadians?" *Association for Canadian Studies.* Retrieved from http://acs-aec.ca/en/social-research/canadian-history-knowledge.

Lenard, P. T. (2012). *Trust, Democracy, and Multicultural Challenges*. University Park: Pennsylvania State University Press.

McDermott, R., and Zimbardo, P. G. (2007). "The Psychological Consequences of Terrorist Alerts." In B. M. Bongar (Ed.), *Psychology of Terrorism*. Oxford: Oxford University Press.

McLachlin, B. (June 03, 2015). "Word of Welcome from the Chief Justice of Canada." *Supreme Court of Canada*. Retrieved from http://www.scc-csc.gc.ca/home-accueil/index-eng.aspx

Nacos, B. L., Bloch-Elkon, Y., and Shapiro, R. Y. (2011). *Selling Fear: Counterterrorism, the Media, and Public Opinion*. Chicago: University of Chicago Press.

Newman, E. (December 01, 2006). "Exploring the 'Root Causes' of Terrorism." *Studies in Conflict and Terrorism*, 29, 8, 749–772.

Perl, R. (March 12, 2007). "Combating Terrorism: The Challenge of Measuring Effectiveness." *Congressional Research Service*. Retrieved from https://www.fas.org/sgp/crs/terror/RL33160.pdf.

Primortaz, I. (2013). "Terrorism is Almost Always Morally Unjustified, but It May Be Justified as the Only Way of Preventing a 'Moral Disaster.'" *The London School of Economics and Political Science*. Retrieved from http://blogs.lse.ac.uk/europpblog/2013/04/29/terrorism-moral-disaster-justified-igor-primoratz-philosophy/.

Silver, R. C. (January 01, 2011). "An Introduction to '9/11: Ten Years Later.'" *The American Psychologist*, *66*, 6, 427–8.

Silver, R. C., and Matthew, R. (2008). "Terrorism." In V. N. Parrillo (Ed.), *Encyclopedia of Social Problems*, (Vol. 2, pp. 926–929). Thousand Oaks: Sage.

Soroka, S. N., Johnston, R., and Banting, K. G. (2007). "Ties That Bind? Social Cohesion and Diversity in Canada." In K. G. Banting, T. J. Courchene, F. L. Seidle, and Institute for Research on Public Policy (Eds.), *Belonging?: Diversity, Recognition and Shared Citizenship in Canada* (pp. 561–600). Montreal: Institute for Research on Public Policy.

Staiger, I., Letschert, R., Pemberton, A., and Ammerlaan, K. (2008). *Victims of Terrorism: Towards European Standards for Assistance*. Report of the European Forum for Restorative Justice.

Swan, D. (July 20, 2010). *A Criticism of Huntington's Clash of Civilizations*. Retrieved from http://www.academia.edu/1416654/A_Criticism_of_Huntingtons_Clash_of_Civilizations.

Waxman, M. C. (February 01, 2012). "National Security Federalism in the Age of Terror." *Stanford Law Review*, *64*, 2, 289–350.

Weinberg, L., Pedahzur, A., and Hirsch-Hoefler, S. (2004). "The Challenge of Conceptualizing Terrorism." *Terrorism and Political Violence, 16*, 777.